FREEDOM IS

Also by Brandon Bays

The Journey: An Extraordinary Guide
for Healing Your Life and Setting Yourself Free

The Journey for Kids:
Liberating Your Child's Shining Potential

FREEDOM IS

*Liberating Your
Boundless Potential*

BRANDON BAYS

NEW WORLD LIBRARY
NOVATO, CALIFORNIA

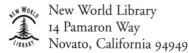 New World Library
14 Pamaron Way
Novato, California 94949

Page 135: Epigraph © Coleman Barks. Used with permission.

Pages 136–37: Lyrics from "The Satguru Song" by Kirtana from *A Deeper Surrender* CD used by permission of Kirtana, Wild Dove Music (www.kirtana.com).

Text design and typography by Tona Pearce Myers

Library of Congress Cataloging-in-Publication Data
Bays, Brandon.
Freedom is : liberating your boundless potential / Brandon Bays.
    p.   cm.
ISBN-13: 978-1-57731-555-1 (hardcover : alk. paper)
ISBN-10: 1-57731-555-3
1. Success. 2. Self-perception. 3. Conduct of life. 4. Introspection.
I. Title.
BF637.S8B375 2006
158.1—dc22   2006012253

First New World Library printing, September 2006
ISBN-10: 1-57731-555-3
ISBN-13: 978-1-57731-555-1
Printed in Canada on acid-free, partially recycled paper

g A proud member of the Green Press Initiative

Distributed by Publishers Group West

10   9   8   7   6   5   4   3   2   1

In gratitude to the
Infinite Grace
pervading all of life

✦

CONTENTS

FOREWORD

Over the past twelve years, Brandon Bays has shared with hundreds of thousands her effective and profound tools for enlightened living and natural healing. I am one of those who has been positively and totally transformed by Brandon's teachings and her organization, The Journey, and I would like to share my personal experience with you.

At one time I would have described myself as fun-loving and jovial with a natural lust for life, but nine years ago my life took an unexpected turn. At twenty-two, during a back-packing trip through Thailand, I was attacked while asleep in my hostel room and raped. I spent five days in a hospital being treated and recuperating.

Afterward, depression took its grip. A year later, I found myself drinking heavily to mask the pain I felt inside and smoking between forty and sixty cigarettes a day. With each passing day I slipped deeper into a black hole of despair, seemingly losing touch with the person I knew myself to be. Although I innately knew that the depression and the attack were connected, no help I sought seemed to work.

Then I discovered Journeywork, the mind-body healing for which Brandon is known. My mother had heard about it from a family friend who was a Journey practitioner, and she invited the woman to come do some work with me. I found the session to be simple and almost effortless, guiding me through layers of familiar emotions that led to a wellspring of love and peace within. My first guided introspection process was deeply profound — for the first time in my life I experienced myself to be everything, the universe. Afterward, I felt a deep sense of peace and a feeling of coming home. Within a couple of weeks, the amount I was drinking diminished, I effortlessly gave up smoking, and the depression began to lift.

Recognizing the possibility of healing, I decided I wanted to attend a seminar with Brandon. During that first Journey Intensive weekend, I came to forgive and let go of my rape. I felt as if a ten-ton brick had been lifted off my shoulders, and I knew I had been given my life back. Ever since, I have continued to soar in freedom.

Brandon's teaching is enlightening and inspirational. Having learned through her own incredible healing journey, in which she healed completely, without drugs or surgery, in six and a half weeks from a tumor the size of a basketball, she empowers us to look deeply into ourselves to find true freedom — emotional, physical, and spiritual. She is a living expression of her teachings, exuding radiance, stillness, and freedom.

Her style is simple, practical, and down-to-earth, yet the revelations she facilitates in us are universal and divine. With step-by-step tools, she enables us to discover for ourselves what many other teachers just talk about: that within us all is deep and eternal stillness, ultimate peace. Many such tools are included in this book. By using them in our daily lives, we are gifted with a direct experience of freedom, and we can begin living our lives as a reflection of our infinite potential, a true expression of grace.

In gratitude for the freedom I discovered, I continued studying at Brandon's various workshops and eventually became a Journey accredited practitioner. I have been continually amazed by the changes I have experienced in my own life and awed at the healings I have witnessed.

With no prior background in mind-body healing, I have been astounded by the body's natural ability to heal. This particularly hit home when I received a call from a twenty-seven-year-old woman who had been diagnosed with breast cancer and a brain tumor. She had a feisty spirit and was determined to participate in her own healing. I partnered with her on her healing journey as she supported herself with healthy nutrition, colonic irrigation, naturopathy, and Journey process work. After three months of continued process work, her brain tumor disappeared. Twelve months later she received the medical all clear for her breast cancer. Through her willingness to turn the flashlight on inside, clear out the old consciousness related to her illness, and learn her life lessons, she was able to participate in her own healing. This type of story has become commonplace in my life.

During the weekend seminars, I have witnessed countless spontaneous healings. I have seen people remove their glasses because their vision has cleared or take out their hearing aids because they can hear clearly again. For others, daily aches and pains or long-term injuries vanish.

The Journey is probably best known for healing deep-seated emotional issues. Witnessing the final healing and resolution of issues as painful as abortion, sexual abuse, depression, divorce, and grief is a miracle. My heart sings when I see clients finally let go of the weight of these burdens and begin living their lives fresh from a place of wholeness and freedom. Often they look as if years have fallen away from them.

I have also had clients whose issues are spiritual; they long to find truth and learn their life lessons. A woman with cancer contacted me in her final days. She asked if I could come visit her to help her find peace and wholeness before she passed. It was a great privilege to facilitate her learning her life's purpose and guide her into the realization of her eternal self. I watched as she forgave people in her life and asked to be forgiven. The peace that filled the room afterward took my breath away. She thanked me, for now she was unafraid to die. Her family told me she abided in the eternal peace that she had discovered until she left the body.

As The Journey has grown organically over the last twelve years, I have toured with Brandon Bays through Europe, Australia, New Zealand, and Africa. In each country, The Journey seems to have its own wings and has taken off like wildfire. Journeywork is now commonly used in hospitals, doctors' offices, prisons, schools, addiction recovery centers, orphanages, businesses, and tribal communities around the world.

Recently, Brandon formed Journey Outreach, a charitable trust that allows The Journey to reach communities that could not otherwise access this work. In 2004 I flew to South Africa to support an outreach project for a government pilot program to use Journey process work in the national school system. The program involved teaching the teachers to use Journeywork and supporting them as they implemented the work with children in classrooms.

Visiting the Zambeni Primary School in a rural district 100 kilometers outside the city of Durban, it was intensely moving to witness the hardships that some of the children face on a daily basis. Many of them came to school with no food in their bellies. Many had lost their families and had no home. Others as young as eight had been the victims of abuse and rape. One child had witnessed his father being murdered. Yet the atmosphere at this school was not one of sorrow; rather, it was full of joy, laughter, and hope. As the teachers began to use Journey techniques in their classrooms, they noticed that the children gained a sense of inner well-being and happiness, their behavioral issues fell away, their academic performances soared, and their true potential began to shine. The principal of the school took me aside and thanked us for assisting. He said that no words could express his gratitude for the positive changes The Journey had brought to the lives of his students, his teachers, and the wider community. Journeywork is now being regularly used in more than 230 schools in South Africa. Outreach programs in Maori communities in New Zealand and Aboriginal communities in Australia have been equally successful.

When The Journey was finally launched in the United States, I was very excited. Being an American, I couldn't wait to share this profound work with my fellow Americans. However, because of timing, The Journey did not experience the same groundswell in the United States that it had in other countries; Brandon's book *The Journey* was released on September 10, 2001 — one day prior to the terrorist attacks on September 11.

Understandably, the launch events and book tour were cancelled. Instead, Brandon and a number of Journey practitioners offered a free seminar in New York for those closely affected by the tragedy. When the hospitals were overflowing with people suffering from physical issues caused by the emotional stress, The Journey provided an alternative path to healing the emotional wounds. It was awe-inspiring to witness people who had been severely traumatized by 9/11 heal and resolve their fear, shock, grief, and anger, enabling them to come to a deep sense of internal peace and well-being, even in the face of such devastation. Since that time, in the United States The Journey has been a slow-building grassroots movement. With the publication of *Freedom Is*, Brandon's teachings become available to U.S. audiences once again.

Within the pages of this book are many profound teachings and practical tools that will effortlessly carry you into the freedom that already is. This book is an answer to the growing prayer from around the world to live a life in freedom and wholeness.

— Laurie Siemers

INTRODUCTION

This book is written to give you a living experience of freedom. It is not designed as a quick read where you simply collect yet more knowledge or anecdotal tidbits. Rather, it is meant to give you a sublime experience of the infinite. It is an invitation to relax, become still, and open deeply into a wordless presence that is here in the spaces between the words.

This presence is your own essence. It is vast, free, and completely whole. It is a huge unborn potential; full of creativity, genius, wisdom — capable of creating anything. It is alive with grace, always here and continuously available. This book provides you with a natural, effortless opening into this exquisite presence, and it gives you the means to clear anything that might obscure your experience of it — in very real, practical, and accessible ways.

This is not a book about grace. This is a book that draws you into it, into the infinite, into the boundless presence of your own inner being.

As you read this book, let it be experiential. Drink in the words, savor them, let them reverberate through your whole being. Take time to bask in the stillness inherent in the spaces between the sentences. Pause for a moment . . . breathe . . . listen with your being. The stillness there is calling you into the embrace of the infinite. This calling is completely familiar to you. It is already known. Your own essence is calling you home.

✦

EACH CHAPTER IS DESIGNED to carry you deeply into a different aspect of your essence. Though in truth there is no one specific word that can describe this boundless presence, there are various qualities that seem to arise from it. As with a rose, even though the fragrance that emanates from it is not the rose itself, so it is with these various aspects of grace. Though grace is wordless, timeless, infinite, and cannot be defined by any one single characteristic, still this presence exudes particular fragrances. The invitation here is to let go and fall into the fragrance of each chapter, letting grace embrace you in its beauty and allowing a deep teaching to arise effortlessly from within.

Following each teaching will be a guided meditation, introspection, process, or contemplation designed to help you open even further — to draw you directly and experientially into the vast embrace. Some of the process work is very in-depth, whereas other contemplations will take only a few minutes. Each and every tool will continue to work on your inner being throughout your day and will cause you to feel a greater level of peace and connection with yourself and others in your life.

The work is practical, usable, and can be introduced into

your everyday life gracefully and effortlessly. Once you've fully experienced the book in its entirety, you might like to begin a daily practice. You can open the book randomly, let your awareness rest on the page, and ask to be guided from within. As you read, let your awareness be relaxed and spacious: listen beyond the words and allow them to do their work, letting yourself fall into the vast embrace of that particular quality of your own essence. As you open, your own deeper wisdom will begin to reveal itself naturally.

As you begin to let this book work on you and transform your life, it will become a living, breathing teaching. You might like to spend fifteen minutes each day and view it as quiet time spent with yourself, letting your inner wisdom reveal new lessons and deeper teachings each time you open it anew. Sometimes as you read a paragraph and pause to let it seep in, your own truth will reveal just how that quality is currently present in your life. Or you might spontaneously experience how it could help heal or resolve a specific situation. Sometimes, as the words settle into your being, you will feel a profound stillness suffused with a crystal clarity, which might have a purposeful, directive quality to it, and you will feel a strong inner guidance. If you feel called to, you can go to the end of the chapter and go through the in-depth exploration or discovery process to deepen your experience and realization.

Each time you open into your own essence will be the first time, for grace is always fresh, always new. Even if you've already dived in and experienced the whole book from cover to cover, each time you open it, the book will reveal something unexpected, something different. Somehow, what arises will be synchronistically perfect for that moment.

No meditation, introspection, or contemplation is ever the same, and as you open into them in all innocence and trust yourself, deeper and more profound wisdom will be revealed. Sometimes this realization will come in words, and sometimes it will reveal itself wordlessly, as a deep inner knowing.

As you learn to open more freely and trust more completely, this book may become a dear friend or spiritual companion calling you back home to yourself, inviting you to experience the embrace of grace that is always here. This book is an adventure, a journey in the truest sense, offering revelations, experiences of the infinite, and clearing process work with guided meditations and contemplations. It is full of inspiring stories, which will continually evoke deeper understanding, and practical techniques that can be applied in all areas of your life.

Ultimately, this book is designed to transform your life into one of effortless ease filled with grace and joy. It teaches you how to apply your own wisdom to everyday situations in very real and simple ways. And it gives you the tools to live your life in gratitude, love, and freedom.

This book truly is a journey within yourself — into the boundless presence of freedom that is what you are.

May you fall in love with this presence, and may the exquisite embrace of grace draw you ever deeper.

1. EFFORTLESS BEING

Effortless being is the sublime presence
that suffuses all fragrances of grace.
It is whole, free, and completely at ease –
and it requires nothing.

Just let yourself relax... trust... open...
and gracefully fall into effortless being.

Let's begin our journey together with "effortless being," as it is the one quality of grace that is intrinsic to and inherent in all aspects of the infinite. Any time you open into the infinite presence of your own self, an effortless presence will have easily and gracefully guided you there. In fact, the only route I know of into enlightened awareness is through effortless being.

So why not plunge in right now? Rather than talk about it, let's experience it directly.

Take a deep breath in, and let it out.

And another deep breath in, and let it out.

Let your whole being relax as you fully put yourself into the scene I am about to describe. As you read, experience it as if it is actually happening right now. Take time in between the sentences to open and *feel* what it would really be like to be in these circumstances. Just imagine that *you* are the person described in this story:

You are in the ocean, out of your depth, struggling to stay afloat. The more you struggle, the less buoyant you feel. Each effort becomes more and more exhausting. Fighting what is, you believe the answer lies in trying harder... reaching, grasping with your whole being, striving with your body, harnessing your mind, trying to focus all of your energy to stay above water — you fight for your life. Your activity becomes frenetic. A sinking futility starts to creep in, but you realize you can't give in, no matter what. You force your mind into high gear. You struggle with all your might. Your striving becomes frantic.

A kind person throws you a life preserver, but it lands just out of reach. Safety is but a few feet away, if only you could grasp it in time. Certain that effort is the only answer, you harness every fiber of your being, desperately trying to grasp the answer to all your prayers, knowing that peace, rest, life itself is just an arm's length away... just out of reach. If only you try harder, the prize of safety, relaxation, freedom will be yours.

But with each fiercely desperate stroke you end up pushing the life preserver farther away. The fight intensifies. You feel your mind starting to spin out of control. You force it into line — everything depends on this final struggle, but your very striving is driving it farther... and farther... and farther away...

Finally, the kind stranger jumps into the water, and when he bobs to the surface, all movement ceases. He appears motionless... as if he is just resting, trusting. Gently, under the surface, his legs flow in the quietest of movements... effortlessly treading water, trusting completely in the ease of grace. As the water becomes still around him, the life preserver freely drifts his way... lap... by lap... by lap. The life preserver finds its way into his relaxed and trusting hands, and with almost no movement — more a softly whispered prayer than an actual motion — he glides it your way.

Still frantic, you grasp for it desperately, but your motion only causes it to drift out of reach again. The desperation becomes unbearable...

You hear a reassuring voice say, *"Relax.* Just *relax. Trust* ... You're safe... All safety is here... Everything you need is *already* here." Then, once again, the kind man who trusts the ocean, trusts grace, softly floats the life preserver in your direction.

As the preserver gets closer, the desire to reach for it becomes fiercely strong. But before you can thrust out your hand, you hear the stranger say again, *"Just relax."*

And something penetrates: it happens in a heartbeat. Against all instincts and conditioning, against everything you believe to be true, you *choose to cease striving*. You relax. You relax your mind. You give up all struggle and relax your whole being. You feel your body softening and, miraculously, the life preserver begins to effortlessly drift your way.

Then, just before it's ready to softly touch your chest, *something happens*. Time stops. Everything becomes still.

Your breathing slows and becomes easy. Your mind softens, every ounce of activity ceases, and your body releases all tension. You become aware that you are being gently supported, embraced in an ocean of trust. In the still center of the silence, you realize all grace is here, surrounding you, supporting you. All peace is here... and you relax deeply in the restful embrace of grace.

You become aware that the life preserver has just tapped you on the chest, and in that instant you realize you don't actually need it. You *never* needed it. You're already safe, already whole, already free. You're floating in an ocean of trust.

Gently, one arm floats to the side of the preserver, and you look around to see if anyone else is struggling needlessly in the water... and *you* become the kind stranger.

A soft smile of irony creeps across your face as you realize the ludicrous insanity of struggling against life. It's like some big cosmic joke. You recognize that everything you seek is already here the moment you *choose to stop the struggle, relax, and trust.* This that had seemed so far out of reach is realized to be everywhere, in everything. And that "something out there, if only I could get hold of it" is realized to be *right here,* as a vast embrace, constantly supporting you in an ocean of presence.

✦

AND SO IT IS WITH GRACE. The more you struggle, strive, fight, reach, grasp, or force your mind, the further away you push the very peace you are seeking. And the moment you stop, soften the mind, relax your body, cease striving, *give up the struggle*, the peace you are seeking is directly experienced to be here as a spacious presence of effortless being.

The very nature of grace is effortless ease. It is already whole, complete, free, vast, and open. It intrinsically knows how to care for every aspect of our lives. It knows the right action in each moment, and it is always in flow. Like a river flowing over water-smoothed rocks, it has a natural ease. Grace is simultaneously supremely restful and scintillatingly alive: it loves to give birth to creation. Yet no one is doing the doing, or "flowing the flow." Grace just *is*. There is no "somebody" who controls, manages, and directs its natural momentum. With effortless ease, it simply flows through life.

As children, so often we heard, "*Try* to do your best." And our focus went to the *trying*. We struggled, we strived, we fought. Had we instead been told, "Relax little one — you are already whole and perfect, and there is a huge potential that is longing to create through you — just relax," we *would* have relaxed, opened, and allowed our genius, creativity, and love to shine. We would have opened innocently and allowed our wisdom to arise naturally, and we would have been delighted to simply be part of the process of creation.

Unfortunately, most of us became conditioned to the idea that struggling is good and makes us strong, and we feel guilty if we take even a few spare moments to relax. But ironically, it is only when we completely let go into full relaxation that true genius and creativity become available.

Have you ever tried to remember someone's name, and

yet for all your efforts, it remained on the edge of your awareness, just out of reach? And no matter how hard you tried, you just couldn't come up with the name? Do you remember what happened next? You eventually *gave up the struggle*, relaxed, and stopped reaching desperately with your mind — and of course, moments later, with your mind now totally at ease, the name unexpectedly popped into your awareness.

So it is with grace. If you force yourself to meditate, setting your mind into a certain groove, focusing on an object, concentrating on words, or repeating mantras, your very efforting will keep away the peace you are seeking. Yet when you just relax, become aware of all sounds, have no purpose other than to close your eyes and "just be" — not caring whether thoughts come or go through consciousness, and letting yourself naturally glide into a spacious awareness — you will find yourself soaking deeply in a restful ocean of healing presence. Then, when thoughts come through, you will find that the stillness remains untouched.

The moment you grasp or grab onto a thought to try to interpret it or understand its significance, all awareness of the ocean drops into the background and your whole being goes to the thought. It's only when you *choose to stop reaching* to analyze the constructs of the mind that you find yourself falling again . . . back into the ocean — the ocean of effortless being. *All* struggle, striving, efforting only takes you away. *All* letting go, opening, accepting, trusting allows you to fall deeper and deeper into the embrace.

Cease all activity and just rest.

Any effort made in meditation just pushes grace away. Indeed, this is true of all life.

✦

I REMEMBER ONCE when I was working with my grandfather in his workshop. Grandpa had a PhD in physics, and he loved to invent things, designing his own creations and bringing them to life with his hands.

I was twenty-three, and I wanted to make a very special Christmas present for my husband. He loved the game of backgammon, and so I went to Grandpa and explained my vision: I had bought some gorgeous fabric from Liberty's in London, and I wanted to use it to build a backgammon set that would allow the beauty of the cloth to be seen. I would have liked to make a glass box, but as that was virtually impossible to manufacture, not to mention impractical to use, I decided to use transparent Perspex. Grandpa always loved a challenge, and he researched the various types of Perspex.

Eventually, he decided the best kind for us was a special brittle version that wouldn't crack or scratch as easily as other types, but he warned me it would have to be handled "with kid gloves."

We spent an afternoon together designing the box, figuring out how to marry the joints so it would be strong and useable, and when the special order Perspex finally arrived, we went down to his workshop to begin constructing it.

Grandpa first bent the Perspex, checking its flexibility and brittleness — to determine its breaking point. He had chosen three different types of saws that he thought would best penetrate the material. After several breaks and misapplied pressure, he scored a perfect line, then he gently slotted in a saw, creating the finest of grooves, and perfectly cleaved off a piece.

It *looked* so easy.

Not wanting to make me feel self-conscious, he casually said, "Okay, I'll leave you to it and go upstairs to see how your grandmother is getting on."

Carefully, I scored the edge, and slowly I lifted the cutting saw. Like Grandpa, I tried to gain purchase with the right angle, but "snap," the Perspex cracked in two.

I took a deep breath. This type of Perspex was expensive and hard to get. I willed myself to get it right: "Okay, this time I'll try harder. This time I need to focus my mind, steady my hand. I will do it right this time."

I held my breath. I scored the Perspex. I steadied my hand and began to saw. It wasn't working. I pushed harder.

"Snap!" Another piece broke in two.

Tears welled in my eyes. I couldn't afford to lose another piece. I mustered all my concentration, all my will, but once again, "snap!"

My head started spinning. Hot tears streamed down my cheeks. I wiped them with the sleeve of my shirt, and with a red nose and a set jaw I went upstairs to Grandpa and admitted that I'd blown it. I just couldn't get it right, no matter how *hard* I tried.

Grandpa smiled reassuringly. "It's only plastic, dear. We can order some more."

"But Grandpa, you made it look so easy."

"Well, why don't we go back down and see what we can cobble together? Maybe I can fix the Perspex — melt it with my torch, sand it, buff it, glue it. Perhaps the crack won't even show. Let's see."

Downstairs, he looked at my botch job and said, "Show me how you're cutting it, dear."

I scored a clean piece, gained purchase with my saw, and just as I began to work it, the Perspex snapped in two again.

Grandpa said, "Brandon, look me in the eyes. Do you see how quiet I become *before* I even pick up an instrument? Now, look how it floats in my hand. You need to think of this saw as if it's a feather that you're stroking through water... softly, easily, effortlessly... Like this."

This burly mountain of a man held the saw delicately, as if it was made of air. He scored a piece with the lightness of a gentle caress and glided the saw gracefully through the plastic. It looked impossible, but the less effort he used, the deeper and freer his movement was. He took my hand and held it, as if holding a small bird. "Like this, Brandon. Less is more. Just let it slide... no pushing, striving. Just let it find its own way. Let the Perspex *teach you* how deep, how fast."

And so it did. And as I effortlessly surrendered into letting *it* teach me, an exquisite Perspex cabinet box brought itself into being.

It's now nearly thirty years since I discovered the power

of effortless being with my grandfather, and in all this time I've never seen a more beautiful backgammon set — ever.

✦

THE POWER AND PRESENCE OF EFFORTLESS BEING actually revealed itself much earlier in my life. I frequently had glimpses or tastes of it, but they were fleeting and mostly passed through awareness unrecognized. Then, when I was twenty-two, I had a very strong taste. I was newly married, and as a wedding gift, my husband gave me the realization of one of my personal dreams. For our first honeymoon night he bought us hugely coveted box seat tickets to a purportedly spectacular performance at the Metropolitan Opera in New York City of the ballet *Romeo and Juliet*, with Rudolph Nureyev as the featured dancer. People had purchased tickets over six months ahead to score a prized seat at what was to be an extraordinary event.

I will never forget that night. It was pure magic. Rudolph danced sublimely, constantly taking our breath away and moving in an exquisite flow of grace. Then, during one of his solos, something unexplainable happened. He seemed to be falling into some glorious reverie as he spun, turned, and pirouetted across the vast open stage. Just as he was preparing to leap into the air, it felt like *time stopped* for a fraction of a second. We all felt it, and the entire audience drew in a deep breath together as everything seemed to come to a complete standstill. Like a great, invisible mantle, all of Rudolph's hard-earned skill and expertise seemed to fall away, and when he leapt into the air, it was as if somehow he had been set entirely free: free to soar like a bird. His strong, athletic body seemed to be made of air as he completely abandoned himself into an effortless grace. For an instant it seemed he was actually floating, and then the impossible happened. His legs reached out, as if expanding like wings, and somehow he lifted infinitesimally higher.

Everyone gasped; my hair stood on end as an unexplainable but palpable thrill coursed through the audience. The leap seemed to go on endlessly — it seemed timeless. Wordlessly, we all experienced it together. One person effortlessly and completely opened into infinite being, and we *all* caught it, felt it ripple through. We tasted the opening.

At the end of Rudolph's performance, the hall became a din of endless cheering, applauding, faces streaming with tears. We could not seem to adequately express our gratitude. We were bursting with joy, and our tribute went on for forty-five minutes — all because we'd been given just a taste of effortless grace.

Truly, it's when we put aside all of our knowing, all of our conditioning, all of our hard work, and cast off all that we *think* we've learned that effortless being is revealed. When we courageously throw off our whole invisible mantle of "the known" — and it's a heavy mantle to carry — that is when we fall innocently into effortless being.

Effortless grace is always here, always available, always surrounding and infusing us. Indeed, it is our very essence. And it is easily revealed when we choose to let go of our ideas of how things *should* be and open into the innocence of the unknown.

From this effortless being, true genius is born, and magic happens.

✦

MY FATHER HAD A DIFFERENT kind of genius than Rudolph's. His genius lay in the fields of science and engineering. During the sixties and into the seventies, my father worked for the U.S. Department of Defense designing and overseeing the building of America's missile-detection radar systems, and he felt weighed down, practically crushed by the responsibility he shouldered.

He was the system's lead inventor and designer, and no one shared his level of expertise or knowledge. If something went wrong in either the conceptual or the building phase, only he had the ability to see and fix it. Knowing this, he would stay up until all hours of the night, poring over calculations on the four-hundred-page data sheets that the cumbersome think-tank computers spat out. When there was an error, and the computer couldn't find it — it was up to him.

At 4 A.M. one night the strain and anxiety became too much. He couldn't find the error, couldn't figure out the answer. Somewhere in those four-hundred-odd pages of data something was wrong, but like a needle in a haystack, it seemed impossible to find.

In despair, he went to bed, and before he fell asleep, he

simply *gave up* altogether. All he could muster was what seemed like an impossibly futile prayer that somehow the solution would be revealed in the morning. For a highly logical, analytical man, this seemed like a ludicrous request, but it was his last thought before he fell into a short and fitful night's sleep.

At 6:45 A.M., my dad's alarm woke him up. Bleary-eyed, he reached to turn it off, when both the mistake and the perfect solution suddenly appeared in his consciousness.

He jumped out of bed, tore through the tall stack of data pages, and found it. There was the error, sticking out like a sore thumb. By 8 A.M. the formula had been corrected, and the new calculations worked out. He went to work with a solution in hand, triumphant that his team of several hundred men could continue to build the radar.

That night at dinner, Dad shared his revelation with the family. Only after he'd put aside all of his knowledge, learning, background, and even his analytically astute mind did the answer arise effortlessly from some deep place in his consciousness. When all striving ceased, all anxiety was finished, an answer became obviously apparent.

When I think of the countless sleepless nights my dad suffered, I dearly wish he'd discovered this secret sooner. And I wish, after such an astounding revelation, that he'd remembered it more often. He made life so hard for himself.

But, like my dad, most of us are conditioned to trust our minds and our thought processes, even after we've had a taste of something deeper. We worship the thoughts coming through awareness, believing them to be real, instead of trusting something *deeper* than our minds, something that only arises in thought-free awareness — grace.

Finding true answers requires that we give up the arrogant belief that our minds have the answers and are in control. Only when we let go into the infinite can grace use our minds as neutral vehicles to transmit knowledge born from the timeless, eternal presence.

Albert Einstein understood this principle. In order to access true genius and formulate the theories that would transform the way we perceive the universe, he said he would close his eyes, relax, and "go into the still, dark place where God is." Though he didn't use our words, his actions were those of one who understood the power of the infinite. Grace gives rise to all genius, all creativity, all answers. His only job was to close his eyes and effortlessly fall in.

Effortless being is the key that unlocks the wisdom of the universe. And it has always been here, always will be, and is always available once *you choose to give up the struggle.*

✦

OVER THE YEARS, I've fallen in love with effortless grace. Whenever the impulse to effort or struggle arises, I instantly grow suspicious of it. I *know*, absolutely *know* in every fiber of my being, that grace is already whole and complete. It requires nothing — certainly not *my* help or efforts. The only one who could possibly feel the desire to struggle is ego itself. And these days, if any tendency to effort arises, I stop instantly and recognize ego is trying to take charge of something. I know that any effort whatsoever will stop the easy flow of grace.

Around The Journey organization, so much manifests in a single year — so many countries are visited, thousands of lives are utterly transformed — that when we look back at all that has taken place in a particular year, we realize that it can only be the flow of grace in action. Even the entire Journey team could not have manifested and accomplished the abundance and richness of results that grace was able to create. It always blows me away to look back and recognize the variety of miracles grace has blessed us with.

So, I'm acutely watchful now: if even a whisper of efforting arises, I instantly realize that it might get in the way of the magical flow of grace that is perfectly manifesting and orchestrating everything, and I stop: I close my eyes, I *choose* acceptance and trust, and I fall into effortless being. Then I pray that grace will reveal the highest action in the right time, and I surrender to letting the divine take the helm and guide the way.

I often joke with people that grace has me tethered on a leash — I innocently follow along and go where I'm led. Then, when all the extraordinary healing, transformation, realization, liberation, and joy is manifesting around me, I know that grace has been in charge. Only the infinite could be responsible for such magnificence. All credit belongs to grace.

For me to take charge, assume control, or take credit for the bountiful miracle of grace's manifestation would be as ridiculous as a twig carried by a torrential river to the ocean taking credit for getting there.

The river of grace is all-knowing, all-pervasive, unavoidable, and relentless, and there is no other choice for me than to surrender, trust, and relax into the infinite.

I pray you will fall so in love with this effortless ease that any impulse to struggle will become an immediate invitation to relax, open, and accept.

Are there ways you've been efforting lately? Have you railed against the way things are? Have you fought against what is, or tried to make things go *your* way, feeling like you're forcing a square peg into a round hole?

Are you fed up with this fruitless and insane game? And are you ready to give up fighting your paper tigers and give in to effortless ease? Then you're ready for a guided introspection.

Guided Introspection: Effortless Being

You can do this process in several ways: You can record yourself reading it and then play it back and follow your own voice (this allows you to relax and close your eyes as you listen to the words), or you might like to do the exercise with a friend, with each of you taking turns reading it to the other. Or you can play the companion CD (to order a copy, see page 221 or visit www.thejourney.com), which has a recording of all the book's process work. Or you can do this open-eyed introspection while reading.

Whenever you read a meditation, whether to yourself or for another, always remember to go slowly, take regular deep breaths, and keep your consciousness soft, open, and spacious.

Take a nice deep breath in...and let it out.

Take another long, slow breath in...and let it flow out gracefully.

Take another long, easy breath in...and slowly breathe it out.

Now, let your awareness begin to open out spaciously in front...Let it become open and vast behind...Feel it expanding spaciously to all sides...Notice the vastness below...and the boundless sky above...

Now just rest as open spaciousness...as a vast, open embrace of stillness...Just rest...

Now, in a relaxed way, scan your body with your awareness...

There are probably some areas that are more tense than the rest. Go to an area where there is a bit of tension and, for a moment, make it even more tense, more tight...Increase the resistance...Now, release it all at once...Breathe into it and feel your breath dissolving any residual tension...Keep breathing long, slow breaths as it continues to dissolve...

Now find another area of tension...Intensify or contract that area...and breathe it out, all at once...Feel it releasing...Surround it with your awareness...Breathe in spaciousness...and release the breath into that area, as the tension continues to dissolve with the out breath...

Keep contracting and releasing until all of your body feels fully relaxed and open.

Now, check your mind. Feel your mind closing like a fist... clamping down, contracting, resisting...Now, with the out breath, blow the tension out...Feel it relaxing, softening, easing...Breathe spaciousness in...and breathe warmth and ease out...Let the tension of the mind relax completely, continuing to dissolve with the breath...

Now, check your being...If there is any holding on, or fighting with life, or resistance to what is, intensify it for a moment... and then sigh it out...Feel your being relaxing...Continue to release as you sigh it out...

Once again, allow all the relaxation to spread: becoming vast in front...free and open behind...spacious and expansive to all sides...infinite below...and spacious and open above...

Just rest now...as an ocean of relaxing presence...deeply vast...

Now, welcome into your awareness something that you've been efforting with, or fighting against lately...Welcome yourself to fully *feel* the tension and contraction you feel when you are fighting with what is...Like the person in the ocean fighting for his or her life, feel the intensity and futility of trying to struggle and resist life...Feel how it affects your body...your mind...your being...Be willing to feel it become even more intense...Fight harder, create more resistance...effort with all your might...

Now, what if you discovered that everything *is as it is meant to be?*...What if you realized that everything that is taking place is happening for a reason and a purpose that you can't fully understand yet?...What if you were to fully, completely, and utterly *just accept what's here?*...

What if it is entirely the will of grace and is out of your hands?...What if there is nothing you can do, should do, or ought to do to fix it?...What if you finally felt what it feels like to completely and totally *relax and accept* that what is here is what is meant to be, in this moment?...

What if, in absolutely accepting, you chose now to *stop struggling...give up...relax*...just relax...let go?...

What if, as you let go, you felt yourself deeply releasing, falling, opening, relaxing into a spacious embrace of infinite presence?...What if this presence was surrounding you, suffusing you...pulling you ever deeper...opening...relaxing...*trusting* ...*trusting*...*trusting?*...

How would it feel to rest in an ocean of trust...just being... effortless being?...

What if you gave up the need to figure it out, find the answers, fix it, change it, make it right?...What if you just *accepted totally* that what is here is what is here?...

Now, just relax in the infinite embrace of pure being...No action needed...No agenda...No desire...No grasping for understanding...

Just this...just this that is here in the abundance of all that is...

And what if you had full permission just to rest and effortlessly not know anything?...How would that feel?...

Now, *just rest, soak, steep* in effortless grace for the next few moments...

With nothing to gain, learn, achieve, or change, ask:"If grace were to take care of this problem, situation, or circumstance, how might it get handled easily, effortlessly?"

And let the question go...Let it go completely...Leave the answer up to grace to reveal in its mysterious way...with its divine timing...when it is ready to...

If you are to be used as a vehicle by grace as a part of some action or solution, the result is not up to you...It's up to grace... No doer...No agenda...No credit taking...Just nonpersonal guidedness...

Leave it in the hands of grace. If you're needed to play some part, it will happen effortlessly...

If you feel efforting arising at *any* time, internally say, *"Stop."* You can even say it out loud. Cease struggling, relax your body, and let grace get on with what it knows how to do perfectly...

Take a nice deep breath in...and let it out...

Take another nice deep breath in...and let it out...

If your eyes have fallen closed, you may open them now.

✦

2. NONATTACHMENT

*When the strings of attachment loosen,
dissolve, and float away,
you are left soaring in freedom
on the wings of grace.*

I learned a lesson in nonattachment that forever changed my relationship with the outer "things" in my life — my possessions, my home, my relationships, my lifestyle, even my own body.

About fifteen years ago, I was sitting in a meditation retreat with an enlightened master who often teaches in the traditional manner, through powerful stories. A particular story impacted me deeply. It crept under my skin and began to infuse my being as a living experience. When, three years later, I was faced with having to let go of everything I held dear in life, I found myself resting in an ocean of wholeness — a wholeness so complete that nothing outside of me could make it more so, nor could anything detract from it. The wholeness was simply completely complete.

When we become attached to something or someone in our lives, most often it's because deep down we fear we wouldn't be complete without them. We fear that if we let certain particular things, people, thoughts, or identities go, we would plunge into the presence of the unknown — alone, lost, and bereft. These attachments are sometimes held so closely that we don't even see them as attachments. They are experienced as our actual identity:

I'm so-and-so's husband (or wife)...

I'm a teacher, engineer, store owner...

I'm from Connecticut...

My family were pioneers...

My children are straight-A students...

I own a certain car/boat/house...

I, I, I...My, My, My...

The things that make up our identity can feel so real that without them we fear we would be nothing. We fear nonexistence.

Even simply asking the question — "Who would I be without my car, job, money, spouse, family, profession, material possessions, home, and friends?" — causes an internal scrambling, a need to cling to something. Nearly everyone experiences some level of attachment. In fact, attachments often feel like an essential part of our individual identity.

So, when some spiritually arrogant youngster, posing as an all-knowing guru or enlightened sage, has the nerve to tell us that the key to freedom lies in nonattachment, we often respond with indignation.

"He's a monk — what does he know about 'true' attachment," we say to ourselves. "I'm not a materialist. It's natural to be attached to your loved ones, committed to your job, invested in your lifestyle, proud of what you've achieved and the possessions you've acquired through years of dedicated hard work. It's *normal* to feel attached to a home you've put all your love and care into. You're *expected* to cherish the knowledge you've spent a lifetime attaining. How could valuing what you've made of yourself and your life keep you from true freedom?"

These are all sentiments I might have agreed with fifteen years ago — until I heard the following story. In the hearing of it, the strings of attachment mysteriously and effortlessly began to loosen their grip and over time melted away naturally. I didn't even know it had happened until I was confronted by a real-life experience of losing everything I loved.

You might like to get comfortable and open your heart, the way small children do when they are getting ready to listen to a favorite bedtime story. Just open your being and relax.

✦

ONCE UPON A TIME, a long, long time ago in India, there was an enlightened master who was also a very wealthy man from a distinguished family and the owner of several factories. He and his devoted disciple were casually strolling through a remote and dusty village one day when they came upon a shop displaying antiques, bric-a-brac, and odds and ends. There, in the shop window, was a totally unexpected item that caused the enlightened master to pause for a closer look. It was a porcelain teacup, sitting all on its own, and when he peered more closely at it, he realized it was the very same, rare, prized teacup he had been looking for for over thirty years. He already owned the first eleven teacups of this priceless tea set, the rarest of its kind, passed down from the rajas of old, and this last cup would make the set complete.

He was thrilled at his great good fortune and felt that grace had smiled upon him on this propitious day, for thirty years is a long time to be searching for a teacup.

Now the shopkeeper, standing in the shadows just out of sight, spied the enlightened master gazing at his window and his heart leapt up into his throat: "My god! He's finally turned up! This is my lucky day. Everyone knows this master is a very wealthy man. Now my wife and I can finally retire. This is the one teacup he needs to complete the rarest set in the world. We've got it made!"

As he gleefully exulted, the shopkeeper told his wife to hide in the kitchen. The gods had smiled upon them, and they could finally close the shop and take their longed-for pilgrimage to the holy city of Varanasi. They could live like kings and would never want for anything again.

As the master approached, the shopkeeper eagerly opened the door, and with a low sweeping bow, he welcomed him and his disciple into the shop. He donned his most ingratiating smile, and with a smarmy, oily voice said, "Namaste, swamiji. How can I help you today?"

The master gently explained that he was interested in the teacup in the window. "Ah, well," replied the shopkeeper, "that is my most precious piece. Perhaps you are aware that it's the rarest of its kind in the world. It belongs to a set of twelve, and it's the last one."

"Yes," said the master, "I'm very familiar with the set. It's a favorite of mine. I'd like to purchase that cup. What is your asking price?"

The shopkeeper's mouth became dry and his heart began to pound. He thought, "This swami knows the unique rarity of the cup. He'll pay whatever I say." In the excitement of the moment, the shopkeeper named an astronomical price.

Upon hearing the amount, the master simply replied, "No, kind sir, I will only pay *this* amount." He named a generous and equitable sum and said, "It is a fair price."

The shopkeeper was taken aback. He had thought the sale would be easier; after all, an enlightened master is not some fishmonger who haggles in the market. Disconcerted, but not too discouraged, the shopkeeper dropped his asking price by half, explaining to the master what a loss it would be to him and reiterating that it was the only remaining one of its kind.

The master acknowledged that it was true. The cup was irreplaceable — the rarest available. Then he repeated the original price he had offered and said, "It is a fair price."

Completely befuddled, the shopkeeper thought to himself in alarm, "Okay, okay. So this master wants to bargain. I'll take it down by half again, but that's it. I'll still end up a wealthy man."

With an unconvincing smile, and no excuse at the ready, he said, "Swamiji, you really do drive a hard bargain. Okay, let me tell you what I'll do. I'll reduce it by half again, but that's it — it's my final offer."

The master's face saddened a little, and in a quiet voice he replied, "I'm sorry, sir. I guess you didn't understand me. I will pay only *this* price. It's a fair price."

He motioned to his devotee that the time had come to conclude their stay, thanked the shopkeeper, and quietly walked out the door.

When they were but fifty paces down the road, they heard someone calling, shouting, and when they turned to look, it was the shopkeeper. He was running after them, flailing, out of breath, pleading, "Swamiji, swamiji, come back, please come back... You can have the cup at your price."

And so they returned and the transaction was completed quite amicably. Of course, the shopkeeper knew that even at the master's price, he and his wife were now set for life. The master knew this, too, and both were well pleased.

While the deal was being concluded and the teacup was being wrapped, the master's devotee noticed a magnificent saber hanging on the wall, just above the shopkeeper's head. He could not take his eyes off it — it was the most intricately designed, yet powerful sword he had ever seen. Whenever he turned from it, he found his gaze constantly drawn back. He felt mesmerized by the sword.

He thought, "I must have it. I'll call it my 'sword of truth.' It will take the highest place of honor in my house, just above the altar. Never before have I seen such a handsome sword. I simply *must* have it."

"I am a man of modest means," he figured, "but if I do exactly what the master did, maybe I can get it at a vastly reduced price."

So, trying to sound very unassuming and a little disinterested, the disciple casually motioned to the sword up on the wall and said to the shopkeeper, "That's an attractive saber you've got up there. I haven't got much use for it, but I'd like to know the asking price."

The shopkeeper looked the devotee in the eye. He was a shrewd man, and though he lived a humble life, he did not like to be toyed with. Pretense left a bad taste in his mouth. Nonetheless, he was feeling pleasantly disposed, having just made the sale of a lifetime, and he decided to be generous, naming an only slightly inflated price.

The devotee feigned a gasp, and said, "No, kind sir, I will pay only *this* price. It's a fair price." He imitated the master to a tee.

The shopkeeper, always happy to barter, for that was how the game was played, dropped the price by half.

The devotee winced, and said, "No, sir. I will pay only *this* price. It's a fair price." And the shopkeeper dropped the price again.

The devotee finally shrugged his shoulders and said, "I guess you didn't understand, sir. I will only buy the sword at *this* price. It's a fair price." And, as the master had now concluded his business, together the two quietly strolled out of the shop.

When they were fifty paces down the road, the devotee looked back to see if the shopkeeper had followed them, but the shop door remained closed. In silence he and the master continued walking. Every so often, the devotee snuck glances over his shoulder, completely nonplussed that the shopkeeper had not come chasing after him. He'd done everything the master had done. Why hadn't it worked?

A mile down the road, they paused for a drink, and the disciple finally spoke up. "Master, why hasn't the shopkeeper come running after me the way he came after you?" The master, a man of few words, remained silent.

"But why didn't he follow us?" the devotee insisted.

Finally, the master spoke. "Do you still thirst for that sword?"

"Well, yes, master," the devotee replied. "Of course I do."

"That shopkeeper can *smell* your thirst. He knows you lust for that saber, and he also knows that when he opens his shop tomorrow morning, you'll be his first customer, and you'll take it at *his* price."

The disciple was silent for a moment, as he let the words sink in, then petulantly asked, "But master, did you not thirst for that teacup? You searched for it for over thirty years. Didn't you crave to complete your set?"

The master was silent, and in the quiet, the student realized that of course the master had not lusted for a mere cup. A little ashamed that he had been so audacious to presume that a master would crave for anything, he humbly asked, "But what is your secret, master?"

The master quietly answered, "He came after me because he knew that I genuinely meant it when I said I would take it only at a fair price — I was unattached. With you he could *smell* your lust, and he knows you'll be back."

"But how can you not crave a cup that completes your rarest of collections?"

"Let me tell you my secret," replied the master. "Every night, before I go to bed, I get down on my hands and knees, and I thank God with all my heart for all the blessings of the day. And then, with my whole being, I offer up to God everything I hold dear. I offer up my factories, my ashram, my homes. I offer up my students, my friends, and even my beloved wife and precious children — in my mind's eye I see the factories and ashram burnt down. I see my family and loved ones taken from me and resting in God's arms. And when my prayer is finished, I go to sleep a poor man.

"When I wake up, I look around me to greet the fresh, new day, and I see God's grace is still surrounding me. And, flooded with gratitude, I get down on my knees, and I thank God with all my heart that for one more day he has blessed me with these priceless gifts. I realize that I am only His caretaker. These gifts were never *mine* to begin with. They have only ever been on loan. *Everything is on loan.*"

✦

EVERYTHING *IS* ON LOAN.

When I heard these words, they had a profound effect on me. They penetrated deeply, and when I arrived home after the meditation retreat, I made a silent vow to myself that I would take this teaching into my life. Like the master in the story, each night I took a few moments to truly thank God for all the blessings of the day, and offered up to grace all that was dear to me — our home, our family, our lifestyle, my marriage, our possessions, and all our material wealth. And I found that each morning I arose with a heart full of gratitude, overwhelmed that I had been blessed for yet one more day.

My relationship to the physical things in my life began

to take on a quality of lightness. I was fully aware that these things really didn't belong to me. They were a gift from grace, and my responsibility or dharma lay in cherishing them, honoring them, and savoring the blessedness of having them around me.

I also came to view my relationships differently. I experienced my relationship with my daughter as extremely precious and a profound blessing, and I felt an even deeper honoring take place in my marriage.

Everything around me began to feel special. Everything seemed imbued with a light, scintillating quality. I became aware of the ephemeral nature of all things — how short a time we have on this planet, and how lucky we are to have the bountiful blessings we are surrounded with. This simple, innocent practice reverberated with ever-deeper teachings about the fleeting nature of existence and how it is our gift to cherish it while it lasts.

I found that an important part of the gift of cherishing what we have been given so graciously is to pass on these blessings to others. Increasingly, I noticed that while the material things in my life came and went gracefully, the completeness and gratitude I was resting in remained untouched. After a while, it became clear there was no ownership abiding anywhere — just life dancing in a vaster context of grace.

A paradox unfolded in my life. There was the profound recognition that everything was on loan and therefore a blessing to be cherished, and yet there was also a totally nonpersonal acceptance of letting the cherished things pass gracefully out of my life and into others' hands if grace so desired. I loved each gift dearly, yet felt completely neutral and unattached in its leave-taking. As a result, I developed both a richer and a *lighter* relationship with the outer things in my life.

Three years after the retreat, I happened to be in New York City for work. I received a phone call from a close friend in California. Our family's home — a modest house on the beach in Malibu — had burned down in a huge forest fire. This house held everything that was materially dear to me — photographs, writing, mementos of family holidays, anniversary presents, inherited porcelain, beloved books, journals, and wedding pictures. Suddenly, eighteen years of accumulated memories were gone, and we were financially devastated and materially wiped out.

I remember so clearly hearing the news and waiting to feel a big thud in my guts... because, of course, the truth was that we would never be able to replace any of these priceless things. We'd lived a modest life to begin with, and we had no clue how we'd get back on our feet and put a roof over our heads again. I kept waiting and *expecting* to feel fear or anxiety over it all, but it didn't manifest!

Instead, I felt curiously light, as if some old karma had been lifted off my shoulders — as if a huge weight had fallen away. All of those things had only ever been on loan, and the gratitude and completion I was resting in felt *completely untouched*.

This fire turned out to be just the beginning of a huge wave of leave-taking that occurred over the next two years (and which I describe in detail in *The Journey*): A year later, my marriage unexpectedly dissolved, my daughter and I became estranged, and the tax authorities ended up taking all our income and savings. Within those two years, everything I had come to know as my lifestyle fell away, and I was left utterly and literally without anything.

And yet, this infinite grace that I was resting in continued to feel so abundant, so full. I can honestly say with my hand on my heart that the wholeness did *not* become less whole. It just became more openly apparent! Of course, the natural experience of grieving, loss, and hurt took place, but it happened within the vaster context of feeling already whole and completely complete.

Over the years since that time, grace has blessed me with new relationships, a new and deeply rewarding marriage, an entirely new and successful business, bestselling books, and a lifestyle so charmed and full of grace that even in my dreams I could not have imagined it. And yet, I'm still aware that *everything in my life is and always was on loan.* I dance an even lighter relationship with the outer things in my life. The gratitude deepens, along with an even sharper recognition that life is truly fleeting and each precious drop of it must be savored. The extraordinary blessedness of everything has only become more poignant.

Truly, nonattachment is your invitation to soar in complete freedom.

✦

ATTACHMENT TO OUTER THINGS is not the only attachment we have in our lives. There is a subtler, equally powerful, and more insidious attachment that happens in our *inner* lives — attachment to our thoughts, acquired knowledge, and learned beliefs.

In addition to whatever training or schooling we've done to achieve success or expertise in a particular field or discipline, our life experience gives rise to beliefs that we may come to hold as truth. We can become subtly attached to these beliefs, which may serve as pseudo-refuge in the known, becoming conceptual security blankets that can seem to reflect concrete reality. When we have the certain belief that our view of the world is the way things really are, we give tacit permission to ourselves to stop investigating life. There's no longer a need to view life freshly because we have our beliefs to fall back on, and our curiosity gets stifled and our natural awe and wonder becomes unavailable.

When this happens, the "known" becomes a dead thing, born entirely from our past references, and we carry it around like so much baggage — dragging our beliefs and certainties along, never bothering to question their continued validity or usability in our lives.

Accepted reality becomes so much dead wood floating around in our minds, and our beliefs become the very prison that keeps us from experiencing freedom, grace, and truth in the present moment.

Indeed, our attachment to this lifeless, outdated, acquired knowledge can prevent us from fully experiencing life. We end up seeing everything through the filters of our beliefs, and as life carries on joyously, miraculously, creating itself anew in each moment, we remain stuck in the old and stale — all because we won't give up our hard-won beliefs.

It's only when we cast off everything we *think* is true, all that we *know*, that freedom finally becomes available in the *un*known. Only when we let go of all our knowledge can infinite wisdom reveal itself.

Here is another beautiful story that has been passed down from teacher to student for hundreds of years. It's an invitation to drop all the dead wood of what we hold to be true and to open into the freshness of the unknown. As you read, allow this inspiring parable to do its work by letting your awareness grow spacious and curious like a child.

✦

ONCE UPON A TIME, there was a great seeker of truth, a man who longed with all his heart to directly experience enlightenment — to have and to embody the wisdom of the liberated masters.

Believing that the masters got all their knowledge from spiritual texts, the seeker set out on a path to know and imbibe every great spiritual text known to humanity. He learned the Upanishads, mastered the twenty-seven thousand verses of the Ramayana, could recite the Vedas, and absorbed all the spiritual knowledge of the Vedic rituals. He memorized each syllable of the Mahabharata. He knew the St. James version of the Bible by heart, and he devoured rare, ancient biblical translations as well. He mastered all the mantras, and the many forms of yoga became second nature to him. He could recite huge tracts of the Koran, and he studied the Torah deeply and fully. Eventually, there was no spiritual book he had not read, no technique he had not learned, no ritual left unexperienced, and no mantra left to learn. By now he was sixty years old, and he was considered the greatest spiritual scholar of his time. No one could better him at a debate; he could overturn any academic argument with some obscure fact retrieved from the vault of his learning. He was thought to be intellectually invincible, and he was immensely proud of all the accolades he had received, the spiritual merit bestowed upon him, and the depth of knowledge he'd acquired.

But in his heart of hearts he sensed, he *knew*, that somehow he still wasn't complete. Enlightenment had eluded him, and as there was no more knowledge he could attain from books, he decided it was time to seek out an enlightened master.

He had heard of an old sage hermited on the top of a mountain in the Himalayas, and though it would be a long and arduous journey, he fervently hoped the sage would give him the final knowledge he needed to be enlightened. So, carrying the necessary supplies and only his rarest, most precious books, he began his trek.

After three weeks and three days, he was only two-thirds of the way there. His baggage had become heavy, and he was growing weary. How could he lighten his load? Item by item, he turned over his scholarly possessions: "Oh, I couldn't give up *that* book — it's the only one of its kind in the world. Oh, and *that* text was given to me as an award for outstanding scholarly merit — I couldn't possibly give up that one." He found that he could throw none of his books away. To him, they represented the sum total of all his knowledge. They were priceless and irreplaceable; they were an integral part of him.

Instead, he began to throw away what other supplies he could afford to lose. This tin cup — he could drink water from a stream in his cupped hands, after all. This heavy plate — he could use a palm leaf as a dish. And he only needed one knife — all other silverware could be discarded. And so, in this way he lightened his load and continued his strenuous journey up the mountain.

Nine days later he finally arrived at the master's hermitage, perched at the very edge of a cliff. Exhausted and weary, he told the master's attendant that he had traveled a huge distance just to receive the final teaching of enlightenment. "Please tell the master I am a learned man, a scholar who has mastered all the spiritual texts, the mantras, and all the Vedas. I do not want to waste his time. I do not need to learn any more texts. I want only to receive the knowledge of enlightenment."

The attendant nodded his head, went to the master's hut, delivered the message, and then returned to the expectant seeker: "The master says he has heard your message, and he will call you when he is ready."

"But I am a busy and important man. I did not come all this way to be put through some rudimentary teaching. There is nothing more for me to learn. I know every text by heart. I'm only here to secure enlightenment. I haven't got a lot of time to waste."

The attendant took the message into the master's hut, and returned with the master's reply: "He will see you when he is ready. He is engaged right now."

Three days passed in just this way: the academic asking for permission to see the master, and the master too busy to see him. Then, when the attendant came back the fourth time to deliver the same message, the academic became exasperated, pushed the attendant aside, strode over to the hut, threw open the door, and stepped straight into the master's room — a simple room, with just a mat and two cushions on the floor.

The enlightened sage was sitting on one cushion boiling water to make some tea. He looked up, saw the man, and said nothing as he returned his attention to his kettle.

The venerated scholar was used to being treated with the highest respect, and he was dumbfounded. He could only plonk himself down on the other cushion and wait for the master to speak. But the master said nothing. He seemed more interested in the tea leaves in his cup than in the man in his hut.

Infuriated, the academician finally spoke out. He began by counting out his doctoral degrees, listing all the spiritual tomes he had mastered, and describing all the rituals he knew. He explained that he was considered the most knowledgeable man in all the land, and that he had only come to the master to receive the knowledge of enlightenment. A busy and important man, he did not want to waste either his own or the master's time with anything unnecessary. He already knew all there was to know. All he needed was the final teaching.

The master listened, and when the man was finished, he turned his attention back to the tea. When the brew was perfect, the master finally said, "Will you join me for some tea?"

Angry, the scholar shrugged his shoulders, agreed to tea, and proceeded to reiterate all he had just said — this time louder and more pointedly, punctuating the more impressive bits with large gestures and putting greater emphasis on the parts of his learning that he felt would make the master understand the urgency and importance of his request.

Again, the master listened but remained silent. When the scholar was done, the master simply put a cup in front of him and began pouring the tea. The cup became full and then began to overflow, the tea spilling all over the dirt floor.

Jumping up so as not to get burned, the scholar shouted, "Master, master! Stop pouring! The cup is overflowing! Can't you see?" The man thought that the sage must have gone batty in his old age.

The master stopped pouring, looked up at the scholar, and said, "Yes, I see perfectly. You are like this cup — so full of your ideas, concepts, knowledge, and learned wisdom that I have nothing to give you. The grace of *true* knowledge cannot flow into a cup that is already full — it would only pour over the sides and go wasted. If you truly want what you say you have come here to receive, take all your precious books and make some *good* use of them: use them for fuel, burn them, for it is cold here. Then take all your awards and certificates and give them to the children of the village to play with, for they are nothing but trinkets — toys for the delight of infants. And then, once your cup is truly empty, we can share some tea together. Then perhaps you'll receive what you came here to experience."

✦

FREEDOM CAN ONLY BE EXPERIENCED in the emptiness of nonattachment: nonattachment to our ideas, beliefs, and acquired knowledge, all of which are merely mental constructs born from the dead wood of our past, and which take our attention away from what is always here — the freshness of the present moment. These constructs act as filters that color and distort reality. When you choose to let go of all you *think* you know, all the filters drop away, and unobscured awareness is all that remains. All enlightenment is realized to be here. It is in subtracting the known that the infinite presence of the *un*known is realized.

Your learned expertise, acquired notions, and accumulated beliefs are like mud on your windscreen of reality — when you take Windex and wash it clean, you are left as crystal clear consciousness, sparkling presence.

It is said that those who *know*, don't know, and those who *don't know*, know.

Resting in all innocence in the willingness to not know *anything*, truth is revealed. *Anything* you are attached to — be it the internal world of mental constructs, beliefs, or expertise, or the external world of relationships, lifestyle, or material possessions — if you collapse all of your awareness into it, will cause you to lose sight of the larger context in which everything appears.

As in the merchant master's story, the secret lies with nonattachment — in the willingness to regard everything in your life as something borrowed, something on loan. The meditation that follows provides a practical first step in welcoming this awareness.

When we live in nonattachment, our life experience does not vanish. Our learning does not disappear, nor our physical world evaporate. These things remain, but we stay wide open and allow all of the play of manifestation to dance lightly through our open awareness. We can delight in our circumstances and experiences, take great joy in them, and yet always remain aware of the vaster context in which they appear. In this way we are neither invested in our outer material world nor collapsed into our inner mental constructs. All is free to come and go effortlessly through consciousness — no clinging, no grasping, no reaching, no identification, *no attachment*.

Just *this*. Open freedom, enlightened presence.

Guided Introspection: Nonattachment

Rather than trying to experience this meditation while reading, it is recommended that you use the companion CD (see page 221), record your own voice, or have a friend read, so that all of your attention can go inside as you listen to these words and contemplate these questions.

In this guided introspection, it is important to take plenty of time to pause between questions to allow your own internal response to arise naturally, in its own time, from the depths of your being. Once you've listened to a question, close your eyes and feel yourself opening to receive a response from within yourself. At first, words might arise, but as you continue to inquire, you might feel yourself falling into a vast, boundless awareness that is wordless, a simple inner knowing. Be willing to experience it however you experience it. Let it all happen naturally.

Enlightened presence is naturally experienced when the bonds of attachment have loosened, dissolved, and been set free. As you contemplate the questions, be aware of any grasping, holding, or reaching for the known, and let go of all resistance. The willingness to experience what remains after the "known" has dropped away is the key to freedom.

Begin by closing your eyes and taking some slow, deep breaths in and out... Allow your awareness to become spacious in front... Feel it become vast and open behind... infinite to all sides... boundless below... and vast above... Let it become vast inside... vast outside... vastness everywhere...

Rest for a moment in all spaciousness, then begin asking these questions, staying open to your own internal response:

If all the things you've identified with in the past — your material goods, your house, your lifestyle — were taken away, what would remain? Who would remain? Who are you without these things?... Who are you *really*?...

If you did not have all your beliefs, mental constructs, ideas, learned knowledge, and expertise — if they all fell away — what would remain? Who are you without these things?... Who are you?...

If you could not define yourself in terms of your job or profession — if all of your training and standing disappeared — who would you be? What would remain? Who are you without these things?...Who are you?...

If you did not have your family — if your parents, siblings, spouse, children, and entire extended family were gone — who would you be? Who are you without these things?...Who are you?...

If your family, background, possessions, knowledge, material wealth, and job never existed, how would you relate to and connect with others? Who would you be? Who would be the speaker? What would speak through you?...Who are you?...

If all the labels that identify and define you dropped away, would there be anyone there? Who would you be? Who are you?...

As you rest in all spaciousness, openly and sincerely ask yourself: Who am I?...

What arises?...

Who are you?...

Who are you *really?*...

What remains?...

Who are you?...

Just rest now in the unobscured presence of your own essence...

All of manifestation is welcome to dance lightly through the vast, open expanse of your own being...

When you're ready, you may open your eyes.

✦

3. PRESENT-MOMENT AWARENESS

*There is a real power in bringing
your awareness into the now.*

*When all of your being is surrendered
to just this moment, fully present,
freedom is revealed to already be here.*

There is great power in the simplicity of bringing all of
your focus, attention, and awareness to the present
moment. Indeed, when all thought has fallen away and all
attention has become riveted in the present, the presence of
grace, of truth, is automatically, instantaneously revealed to
be already here.

It is a great mystery as to why this is so, but it is true
nonetheless. As a matter of fact, if we explore the principle
using our own direct experience, it becomes so apparent, so
evident, that it's astonishing we could have ever overlooked
this simple, profound truth. When you bring your awareness
to the moment, freedom is realized to be already here.

Why not try an experiment? Right now bring all of your awareness to just this tiny moment: No thought of past. No thought of future. Just *this* moment...

Let your attention rest effortlessly on the words you are reading... Notice what the letters look like... Feel the weight of the book... Feel the thickness of the page... Notice the faint scent of the paper or the smells in the room...

Let your being settle. Know that for this tiny instant all awareness can gently come to rest in just *this moment*. If there are sounds in the background, let yourself relax in the awareness of them... Take your time... *Just be present to this moment.*

If you find your mind is straining, or efforting to focus, soften the tension or contraction in your brain. Let your awareness become aware of any opening or closing going on in the mind. Let your awareness remain vast and open without any desire to change anything; if you do, the contraction or tension of mind will relax and open naturally. Just stay wide open and notice how mind feels as it relaxes and opens...

Now become aware of what the mind is appearing *in*. Become aware of awareness itself... What is body appearing in?... What are thoughts appearing in?... What are emotions arising in?... Be still and present to *just this moment*.

What is here?

If you are really just *being* here now, in this moment, with no thought other than of awareness being riveted to this instant, you will become aware of a stillness inherent here...

a vastness... a spaciousness. It's always here. Freedom always is. Yet we often put our awareness everywhere *but here*. Presence can only be experienced when all awareness is riveted in this moment.

.✦.

FOR CENTURIES, YOGIS HAVE RECOGNIZED the power of a still mind riveted in the present moment, and they have tried to harness the attention of the mind by *forcing* it to focus on the divine, or a deity, or a specific object. They have written volumes on how to train the mind to become still by attending to specific sounds or repeating certain mantras or prayers. They have taught their students how to focus on candle flames, asanas, chakras, and inner lights in an attempt to still the constant motion of the so-called monkey mind, and thereby experience infinite stillness, mind-free awareness. In other words, they try to use the mind to still the mind.

While it is true that when "mind talk" slows down and falls away, open, free awareness is revealed to be already present, it is equally true that this very forcing, training, efforting, willing, cajoling, and judging of thought can push the experience of freedom further and further away, so stillness continues to elude us. One cannot use mind talk to stop mind talk — for as soon as the will relaxes, all thoughts naturally come flooding back into consciousness. It's like trying to use a dirty cloth to clean up a mess. You just get a bigger mess.

What if there was nothing wrong with the mind? What if *resisting and judging* our thoughts was the true mistake? What if wishing the thoughts weren't there and trying to will them away — or worse, battling with them, trying to overcome them with willpower, sounds, mantras, or affirmations — was the real problem?

What if our thoughts have no meaning whatsoever, except the meaning we choose to give them? And what if we realized that thoughts are really just a bunch of syllables trailing though consciousness? Can you get a sense of how giving energy, attention, will, struggle, and import to thought only perpetuates the very thing we wish to be free from? It's a futile, counterproductive venture.

Instead, what if your experience was of being an open sky of awareness, effortlessly resting in the moment, giving your full attention to whatever is here in front of you now? What if thoughts were allowed to waft through awareness *without* you engaging in or attending to them? What would that be like?

For me, it creates a keen alertness, a spaciousness, a present moment–ness as thoughts waft through the open sky of awareness like a flock of birds. I can hear their distant call, but the open sky is untouched by the noise or the movement. My attention is riveted in this moment — effortlessly in the now, and the birds are none of my business. Awareness is simply aware that they've flown through.

It feels relaxing, true, open. And it is totally effortless. Any efforting is an invitation to *stop*, open, and be present.

But the truth is that most of us *like* to be entertained by our thoughts. We find them fascinating. Maybe we believe our own story of past pain, injustice, or hurt. Maybe we believe our victim-ness defines us. Who would we be without all the stories of the past to examine and reexamine, add to and perpetuate? We believe they give us meaning and context.

But what if that were all just a lie? What if our past was just that — *past, gone?* The reality is it's *not* here right now. In order to bring pain, torment, and hurt forward, you have to *choose* to welcome them into your present awareness, then you have to feed the flame of that pain, add fuel to the fire, using your thoughts to enhance and heighten a pain that is not even here as part of the present moment.

Only *this* moment is here, and thank goodness, life loves you enough to give you the choice each moment: Do I follow my thoughts, lay a nice feast for them, give them my energy, my attention, add color, flavor, spice to them, make them all-important? Or do I stay as open sky, notice thoughts coming through awareness, pay them no heed, feeling that they truly are none of my business, and allow them to come and allow them to go?

Open sky is *not* touched by what comes through it.

However, if we pluck those birds out of the sky — feed them, admire them, imbue them with our love, trap them, hold them, and decide they give our life meaning, and worse still, when they fly away (as they inevitably will, because thoughts are merely fleeting experiences that last only as long as we hold them in our consciousness), if we give ourselves permission to use them as weapons to blame others, or life, for the pain we're in — we can fuel our story of suffering in perpetuity. We can even make a lifestyle of our story, calling our friends to gossip about our thoughts and enlisting their support in blaming others for them. Or we can go to therapists to pull them apart and analyze them, until we are consumed by "me and my story of pain." Then the worship of thought becomes our religion, our identity, our life.

Or, we can just *stop the game.*

I have a definition of free will that is based in science. In recent years scientists have found that *before* any thought gives rise to itself there is a momentary pause, a tiny gap, which occurs just before we become conscious of the thought. In that split second we have a choice: Do I follow the thought and give it all my attention, or do I *stop* and remain riveted in the present moment, allowing thought to give rise to itself and flow unattended through open consciousness, like so many distant birds soaring through the sky?

The choice is yours, and it is available to you each and every moment. What you choose is up to you. This is a true definition of free will. You are free to follow your thoughts, creating self-induced pain and drama, and you are free to allow thoughts to effortlessly come and go, letting them be none of your business.

Over the years I have become so bored with my thoughts, so tired of my story, that nowadays when thoughts come, it feels like too much effort to even bother to listen to them, to take notice of them, or even believe in them. I just don't believe in the story my mind creates anymore. I know mind talk is just a string of syllables coming through consciousness, and it has *no* significance other than the significance I choose to attribute to it.

The fascinating and wondrous thing is that, because I am so disinterested in thoughts of the past, and even less interested in constructing painful imagery of the future, my thoughts have become bored with *me*. They realize I am not going to feed them, be seduced by them, or give them any energy, and so they often don't bother showing up at all. They realize they're not going to get my attention because I genuinely don't believe they have any meaning. So, long periods of time are spent in thought-free awareness. Not because I willed it, or concentrated on mantras, or repeated affirmations, or forced or trained my mind, but because I offer thoughts no resistance. I just can't imagine what entertainment value being made miserable by my self-chosen thoughts might have. So, innocently, I rest in thought-free consciousness, and because my thoughts are bored with me and I'm bored with them, they don't bother arising.

Thoughts are free to come, thoughts are free to go — effortlessly. And you can just rest as the open sky of awareness itself. It's so freeing, so easy.

Guided Introspection:
Welcoming All Thoughts

Why not try another a quick experiment? As with the end-of-chapter meditations, this short guided meditation can be found on the companion CD (see page 221), or consider recording your own voice so you can experience it without reading.

Close your eyes and gently become aware of awareness...

Allow yourself to become aware of how open and vast the awareness already is in front of you...How spacious and free it is behind...How vast and open it is to all sides...It's just free...

Now, staying *as* this, put out an "all call" to *all thoughts* — really put out a huge welcome — welcome all thoughts to come flooding into the vast open sky of your awareness...

You can let it become a veritable din if need be, but just allow them all to come...You can even welcome not just your thoughts but all the thoughts that have ever existed...even all of humanity's thoughts.

Stay wide open and relax your body as you allow any and all thoughts to come pouring through consciousness...Stay still and open...Does any thought really touch the essential you?... Does it in any way affect open sky?

✦

MANY PEOPLE WHO TRY this guided introspection for the first time often find themselves so at ease, so welcoming, so vast, and so open that *no thoughts* even bother showing up.

This is a secret, a mystery. When no resistance is offered to thought, when all thoughts are fully welcomed, thoughts realize they are finally free to come or *not* come — they realize you are *not* going to resist them or engage them in a battle. Usually, they feel so welcomed that they just rest undisturbed, and awareness remains open and free.

Sometimes, the first time you try this experiment a whole host of thoughts come flooding. If that is the case, just admit the truth of your experience. Do these thoughts in any way touch, affect, or alter freedom? Or does freedom, does spacious awareness, remain untouched by anything that comes through it? If you are open and honest in the experiment, you will notice that the essential you, presence, is absolutely untouched by *anything* that comes through it.

So the choice remains: Do I choose to pull thoughts out of the sky, invest them with my energy, time, and life force, and let my self-created, self-induced pain and drama be enhanced? Or, do I allow thoughts to come and allow thoughts to go, and just stay as open sky, in freedom?

The choice is yours, and it's always available. It's the true definition of free will.

✦

OFTEN WE PAY HEED TO OUR THOUGHTS not to add drama or pain to our life, but because finding answers is just plain fun. We want to understand why things happen, know what we should do, and imagine what the future will hold. Rummaging through our past experiences can be fascinating, but the truth is the thinking mind can only give rise to answers we already know or have learned. It can only give conditioned responses. The thinking mind is a trained animal, and it follows the rote, learned formulas we teach it. When we worship the acquired mind-talk born from our thinking mind, our awareness collapses into the known. We have pat answers for everything. We "knee-jerk react" our way through life.

On the other hand, *infinite* mind is an unborn potential capable of giving rise to true genius, inspiration, and free thought. For true inspiration to arise we must open and *stay* open *freshly* in the *un*known. To do this, we must be willing *not* to know, not to have the answers ready-made for regurgitation upon command, not to resort to or fall back on known formulas, idioms, or set cultural beliefs. We must be willing in *each moment* to rest easily in innocence, to be fully present to *this moment*, which can never be known in advance. We must be freshly open to what life is revealing in each moment.

This entire book has been written from this open presence. I have not known in advance what was going to write itself onto a page. Even in the writing of that last sentence, I did not know what would fall onto the page until *after* it was written down.

It takes courage to be willing *not* to know. And mainly it's a decision, a choice. Innocence and present-moment awareness are one and the same. To be totally open to this moment means not to consult our past ideas about what it might mean, nor to look to the future for what it could mean, but to be just here now, in what is here in this instant. Then the next moment will come, and we are present to it. And the moment after that arrives, and we are freshly open to it. Life then becomes a never-ending stream of moment-to-moment *nowness*. Always here, always now.

My dear friend Catherine Ingram, a beautiful spiritual teacher and author of the book *Passionate Presence*, has developed a wonderful metaphor that I find useful in staying present to the moment.

A favorite question of the thinking mind is to ask "Why?" Of course, asking why will only lead us into an endless morass of seeking and confusion, questioning and wondering. And it takes us directly out of what is being revealed right here, right now. When a why question arises — like, "Why is the sky blue?" "Why did a picture of my mom just come through awareness?" "Why is that person doing that?" "Why can't I get it right?" and so on, ad nauseum! — it takes us directly into mind and out of the moment.

Catherine likes to suggest that we use an imaginary bucket — what she calls the bucket of unknowables, and which I sometimes refer to as a mystery bucket — and throw all our why questions into it. "Why is the sky blue?" — Don't know, in the bucket. "Why did my mom's picture just come through consciousness?" — Don't know, in the bucket. "Why can't I get it right?" — Don't know, in the bucket.

It's so simple, yet so powerful. Honestly, sometimes it feels like my whole life is in the bucket!

Why not try it for yourself right now? Releasing why questions into the unknown allows you to keep all your awareness right here, right now. Simply ask a why question. Now immediately reply, "I don't know," and imagine tossing the question into the bucket of unknowables. Can you feel how easy and freeing it is?

Some of you might be thinking, "Yes, but how am I going to *know* what to *do* in any given moment?" My experience is that the *infinite* intelligence knows *exactly* what to do each and every moment, and not only that, but it has an uncannily divine appropriateness to its knowing. It knows

how and when to brush your teeth, add up the numbers on
your tax form, care for your child, and file your papers at
work. When you bring your full attention to *whatever* you
are doing, be it washing the dishes, listening to a friend, or
working on the computer, in the stillness grace will find the
appropriate response, answer, or action. But endlessly asking
"Why this?" and "Why that?" only takes us out of the
moment, and we become less efficient, less elegant, less graceful, and sometimes totally ineffectual.

I was recently talking to Tricia, one of our staff members,
and she was telling me how powerful a "killer of action" it
is when you take your awareness from the present. She said
that when there is lots to do, if she lets her awareness be
drawn to catastrophic pictures of the future (seeing herself
becoming overwhelmed and unable to cope with her work)
or if she lets her awareness drift back to remember her past
struggles or failures, she can become so overcome with the
impossibility of it all — feeling the guilt from the past and
incapacitating fear of the future — that her awareness collapses completely and her body goes into shut-down mode.
Then nothing gets done.

She said that her new strategy for freedom is, the moment she recognizes this old pattern, she sees through the
game and chooses to stop; she brings her awareness right to
the moment and gives all of her love and attention to the task
in front of her. Effortlessly and instantly she becomes present. In being present she finds ease, grace, freedom, and
absolutely *no* stress whatsoever — and activity takes place
efficiently, effortlessly.

Stress is born from our willingness to take up residence in debilitating pictures of the past or from collapsing our awareness into imaginary limiting pictures of the future. The good news is you have a choice. You can decide to reside in the stress or step into the magic, beauty, and elegant efficiency that is here when all awareness is riveted to the *now*.

Freedom is a choice.

So, if a "why" arises, just *stop*. Say, "Don't know," and throw the question into your bucket of unknowables. Simply bring your awareness back to the task in front of you. The freedom and release you feel will astound you.

✦

I RECENTLY HAD A POTENT AND BEAUTIFUL REMINDER of the magic of what grace can accomplish when your being is riveted and surrendered into the timelessness of the present moment. Even in the most pressured and hectic circumstances, if you are willing to give all of yourself to the moment, miracles can happen.

Over the past few years it seems that my seminar schedule has become increasingly booked. I teach forty-four out of fifty-two weeks in a year, with writing, media, press, and family holidays slotted into the few remaining weeks. And it's not just how much time is devoted to offering the work, but how much traveling is required. I am on an almost constant global teaching tour that often takes place at a breathless rate.

But I can only be in this moment, right now. I find I can't afford to drag the previous moment into this one, and I don't have the time or energy to contemplate what could, should, or might take place in the future, for it would only scare me to see the magnitude of it all.

So, my job *requires* me to stay present to what's happening here, right now, in this moment. Any deviation from the now would only spin me into a huge energy drain.

This was never more evident than recently, when I agreed to be the celebrant and to host at my private home a wedding ceremony for Maarten and Yvonne, two young Journey team members.

I arrived home from my summer holidays and had to hit the ground running, since I had only a single "preparation week" before leaving on a new worldwide seminar tour. This week was to be a whirlwind of back-to-back meetings, a presenters' seminar, staff meetings, teaching, and vision-questing, and the wedding was scheduled to take place in the middle of it. But this was an occasion that required a real honoring and reverence. Despite all my seminar obligations, I couldn't just put it on the back burner and then squeeze it into a space between other equally demanding events.

If I'd allowed my mind to fall into the trap of envisioning all my obligations and upcoming events, I honestly feel I would have collapsed under the sheer weight of responsibility of all that lay ahead of me. But there was no time to dwell on what was not yet here, nor on what had just taken place. In reality, there is only this moment, right now.

We often have the belief, "If only I didn't have such a hectic schedule, if only everything were under control and in its place, I could take *time out to be present.*" This is a notion that puts you on a path of postponement, and it is actually completely untrue, unreal. Because, if you are fully present, even in the face of a whirlwind, grace manages appropriately and effortlessly to take care of all aspects of manifestation. When our minds dangle wastefully on thoughts of the past or dwell in pictures of the future, our awareness is not focused and present to what is here right now. The task at hand takes twice as long because the mind is wandering elsewhere.

During my preparation week of seminar meetings and workshops, the bride and groom came over many times to consult with me about food, music, rental of equipment, timings, programs, ushers, vows, readings, shopping, dress code, flowers, decoration, the outside pavilion, seating — you know what weddings are like, the list goes on and on. These meetings had to be sandwiched in between my other business commitments, all of which were necessary, important, and impossible to change. Yet in each meeting with Maarten and Yvonne, there was a timelessness as we effortlessly addressed the needs of the moment, taking time to offer our love and energy, opening our beings to allow grace to give rise to the inspiration needed to create a graceful, elegant wedding ceremony. Circumstances required me to stay completely riveted, patient, and present to the myriad needs of the bridal couple.

As the wedding day came closer, more action needed to

take place: food to be purchased; plates, glasses, tablecloths to be hired; flower arrangements to be agreed upon; printed programs to be made; music to be organized, and so on. This was not something that could be fobbed off on someone else. Each item had to be addressed, honored, and accomplished appropriately.

On Saturday, the day before the ceremony, a number of the Journey team and staff pitched in to help, and they too effortlessly fell into action. You might imagine that — since I was host, wedding organizer, caterer, decorator, and officiant for the sacred celebration happening on Sunday — at some time I might have given myself at least momentary permission to collapse in exhaustion under the pressure. But time did not allow for such indulgences. Complete surrender was the only option. And a remarkable, almost magical, phenomenon began to occur throughout Saturday. Outwardly, to all those who entered the house, it looked like a maelstrom of chaos, a hurricane of activity: I actually overheard a delivery person say, "It's like a circus in here." But somehow everyone was surrendered, lightly carrying on, going about the tasks of cooking, cleaning, decorating, arranging, and miraculously turning our home into an exquisite chapel, a sacred, glorious sanctuary for the wedding.

In the midst of this hurricane, time felt as if it was beginning to stand still as I sat quietly, patiently with the wedding couple and meticulously and lovingly went through every final detail of the wedding day. I felt so open that it was as if everything and everyone around me was welcome in the embrace of that openness. *There was no resistance anywhere.*

We were frequently interrupted as my attention was drawn to oversee the flower arrangements or to make some decision on everything from the placement of the pavilion, to the arrangement of chairs and cushions, to where guests should park their cars. Someone asked if the bruschetta needed more spice. Someone else needed to know how to operate the sound system.

Yet, curiously, amazingly, there seemed to be so much time. It actually felt like time expanded — that it was leisurely and gracious, and there was plenty of time to answer all questions and make all decisions while remaining open, patient, and honoring of the wedding couple. It felt so spacious that there was even room for new inspiration for the ceremony to spontaneously give birth to itself. And it's no surprise that the following day the wedding turned out to be glorious, sublime, absolutely infused with grace. All because total surrender to the moment allowed grace to flourish.

Recently I've begun to wonder if, when we surrender all of our being, consciousness, and love to the moment, perhaps time becomes illusory and grace takes over and begins doing the doing. Of course I can't know if this is true, but it is what it feels like.

Nature abhors a vacuum, and when you offer all of yourself to the needs of the moment — all of your thoughts and emotions, your being — when you surrender everything, it is as if this leaves an emptiness, a void, and grace rushes in to fill the gap and does all the doing through you, as you. All I know is that it feels effortless — like being made of air, lightly dancing in freedom. And it feels like no one is doing the doing. Somehow, life is dancing itself.

The invitation is to just *stop*. *Stop* making excuses as to why you cannot be present. *Stop* entertaining thoughts of past or future. *Stop* asking why or how. *Stop* resisting the endless motion and activity of life. *Stop* protesting, "But there's so much to do." *Stop* resisting the way things are.

Simply stop.

The bliss of freedom is waiting for you, and it's revealed to be here the moment you give *all* of yourself to the *now*. The time has come to stop and open your whole being to life. The choice is yours. The discovery awaits you.

Freedom already is.

Guided Introspection: Releasing and Forgiving Self-Judgment

Here is a powerful process for releasing self-judgment. The truth is that most of us are secretly very hard on ourselves, but self-judgment distracts us and keeps present-moment awareness at bay, taking us out of the now. It can act as a shroud, veiling the beauty of just this moment.

If your mind talk is full of continual self-criticism, I find the best way to handle it is to bring it out into the open, acknowledge the game, and finally forgive yourself for being such a harsh judge. When judgment is understood, forgiven, and let go of, then all of your being is free to settle simply and easily into just this moment.

*Being here in the moment becomes easy, obvious, and the beauty
and grace inherent in the now is effortlessly exposed.*

*For this guided process, I suggest following along with the com-
panion CD (see page 221) or with your own recorded voice, or have
a friend read this to you, so that you can listen comfortably with your
eyes closed.*

Begin by closing your eyes and taking a few nice deep
breaths in and sighing them out... Let your breath become slow
and even.

Then become aware of your awareness... Experience how
spacious it already is in front... How vast it is behind... Feel the
expansion to all sides... and just rest in a bath of stillness.

Now, in your mind's eye, imagine a campfire. The nature of
this campfire is unconditional love, all acceptance.

At this campfire there are only two people. There is a younger
you, who can be any age from zero right up to yesterday — so a
flexible age range younger you.

Then there is the present-day you who has previously been
full of judgments, blame, and self-criticism.

If you look deeply at the younger you, you will see that the
younger you feels so diminished, wretched in fact, for it seems no
matter what the younger you did it was never good enough. And
even when something did come out okay, there you were ready
to point out how it could have been better.

The younger you has been made to fit the mold, to measure
up to everyone else's harsh standards, and yet it seemed no matter how hard the younger you tried they just didn't measure up.
They just weren't good enough.

Amid all this blame and judgment, in the face of all the internal criticism, the younger you lost sight of who they really were.

They forgot the beauty, the magnificence, the grace of their true self, and instead they tried to fit into everyone else's idea of how they should be. And still it was never enough.

If you look, or sense, or just know, you'll see the younger you feels wretched, weighed down, in despair. So begin this campfire conversation by saying out loud to the younger you:

"I am so sorry for all the judgment...I've been so hard on you. No matter what you did, no matter how hard you tried, it was just never good enough for my impossibly harsh standards...I tried to make you fit the mold, and when you couldn't get it exactly right, then I judged you some more...I've been so hard on you.

"I'm so sorry...I forgot that inside you is a real beauty, a real grace...Instead I bought into everyone else's ideas and concepts of how you should be, and I lost sight of the *real* you...I'm so sorry...Please, will you forgive me?"

Now open your own chest, as if opening a suit of armor, and allow all the forgiveness from the younger you to penetrate into the body and being of the present-day you...Take your time and really open to receive the forgiveness for all your judgment.

Then turn to the younger you and say, "I'm so sorry I lost sight of the real you and tried to make you fit the mold...cruelly judging you when you didn't get it right...I promise to stop this blame game starting now...I forgive you for all the times you didn't measure up to my impossibly harsh standards."

Now open the chest, the armor, of the younger you and see and feel the presence of forgiveness and loving acceptance permeate the younger you.

While that is happening, say, "I'm so sorry for the past...and from now on I'm going to see the light in you, the love in you, the simplicity of grace that is your essence."

Now imagine lifting the garment of pain and judgment off the shoulders of the younger you, taking that old coat of judgment and throwing it into the fire.

Now give the younger you some balloons. In the first balloon is self-love...Let the younger you breathe in self-love now, and let it suffuse and permeate the younger you...Now give a balloon of self-acceptance...Breathe that in...And give a balloon of knowing you are the presence of divine being...Breathe that in and let it imbue and permeate the younger you.

Imagine turning to the younger you and repeat the words, "I'm so sorry for all the previous pain and judgment...From now on I will love and protect you and begin opening into the extraordinary essence of grace that is our nature...You are a beautiful being, full of magnificence and truth."

Hug the younger you and let the younger you merge into the present-day you, growing up now in the embrace of self-acceptance, self-love, and self-knowledge and in the realization that you are grace itself and perfect just as you are.

Now, once again, allow awareness to expand spaciously in front...boundlessly behind...open to all sides...infinite below ...and spacious above. Just rest as an open sky of all acceptance.

And when all parts of you are fully integrated and ready to begin living from this consciousness of freedom and self-acceptance, you'll find you'll be able to open your eyes and be present to the here and now.

When you are ready, open your eyes now and rest in a bath of self-acceptance.

✦

4. HONORING AND REVERENCE

Honoring and reverence –
the wings of grace.
With them you
soar blissfully in freedom.

Reverence is a fragrance of grace that arises only in all innocence and complete freshness.

Reverence is not a word that immediately comes to mind in the context of freedom, and yet, when you are resting in the presence of grace, you cannot help but feel a natural reverence for the magnificence of all creation shining around you. It arises spontaneously as the heart overflows with gratitude for the beauty of what is — just this moment.

Yet this reverence is only available as a natural expression when you are fully *in this moment*, without any thought of the next moment and without any dragging of the past into the present. It is available when all comparison falls away and when all expectancy has dissolved.

I had a strong experience of this one balmy summer's eve on the island of Maui. The sun was just beginning to set as I stood on the docks having an idle conversation with my dear friend Becky after what had been a long, lazy day on a boat that had listed and lulled a little too much for my tummy. Queasy and grateful to be standing on the stable surface of the docks, I was letting my body find its own equilibrium as Becky chatted and engaged my full attention.

As she spoke, a flash of orange light reflected off her sunglasses, and this snapped me out of a somewhat sleepy lull and into a sharp awareness of that instant. I mentioned to Becky the gorgeous apricot-colored light glinting off her glasses, and together we innocently turned to see, on the horizon, the sun getting ready to dip into the ocean — like a fiery, blazing red-orange ball. The sky was shot through with corally wisps of cloud, strewn across clear turquoise, which looked soft in comparison to the now deep watery-navy blue of the sea. A long, trailing orange glow reflected in the ocean, sparkling where it caught the tips of waves, creating a glistening ripple in the shimmering liquid light.

We both gasped. It took our breath away. Tears came spontaneously to my eyes as I stood in a reverie, lost in the moment, unable to speak. In silence, motionless, we watched the spectacular display of colors transmute into deeper and more intense hues, until finally the sun dipped fully behind the horizon and disappeared altogether.

An eternity took place. All was silent except for the gentle lapping of the sea as it slapped the docks and receded.

Turquoise faded into indigo, as a huge mellow moon appeared and a cool breeze wafted through. Everything became totally still.

My heart, overwhelmed with the glory, felt like it might not be able to hold such beauty. The immensity was too much. I felt I might burst with the exquisiteness. All reverence for life flooded consciousness — gratitude for what is... pure gratitude. Tears streamed down my cheeks. It felt as though we'd *always* stood on this dock, that we'd only ever been here — the moment lasted forever.

The next night I decided to go out to the same dock, hoping to experience the same magnificence, to taste the same true reverence. Sadly, try as I might, it just wasn't the same. I was "looking" to repeat the experience of bliss from the previous night, but my very expectation, my longing, prevented me from experiencing the simple, more subtle beauty that was shining everywhere on this sweet summer's evening. This night was a "pastel" type evening, and lovely as it was, the moment seemed flat in relation to the night before. Somehow, the feeling of being graced just wasn't there; true reverence was missing.

Thinking that somehow I could call it forth and invoke it into existence, I closed my eyes. With all my being I pictured the previous night in all of its splendor. Hoping to feel the goose bumps that had come with the thrill of bliss wafting through, I only got a less heightened experience. Like looking at a picture in an old family album, it had all the right images, but it wasn't alive, fresh, new. I just couldn't *make* reverence happen.

There I was, standing on the docks, looking at a panorama

of paradise, yet I couldn't see it because I was too busy *comparing* it to my past experience. Seeing the moment through the filters of the past, I could only get a partially obscured view of the present.

I was *over*looking the immensity of glory that was showing up right here, right now — showing up differently — with different colors, different clouds, different smells. But because it did not match what I had come to believe was the ultimate sunset, I couldn't feel the natural omnipresence of grace surrounding me, and I left disappointed.

The next night, I ended up staring out to sea, *not expecting* anything. Grace had let me down. After all, it had only been a faded moment of glory, which disappeared into the sea — a fleeting glimpse of the divine. I turned my focus away from the ocean, and let my toes sink into the sand. As the sun began to set, I noticed how the shadows lengthened, and the sand quite suddenly grew cooler. A rough, broken shell was toying with my big toe and a bubble appeared in the sand, as the sea quietly snuck up on me and tickled my feet with its foam, then receded back into itself. Like a child, totally unexpectant, I lost myself in the tiny details of the moment, and a quiet, almost imperceptible bliss began to bubble up from somewhere inside. As I gazed at the sand, I noticed that the broken whitewashed shell was turning pink, and when, innocently, I looked up, I was arrested — the sun was just getting ready to set over the ocean, and the beauty took my breath away. My heart burst in gratitude and reverence, for the magnificence of life was everywhere.

Not wanting to compare, or cling to, or memorize this

moment in any way, I just rested in open reverence until the sun glided into the sea and disappeared.

It left me in a sweet stillness, and when I came home that night, no talking was needed. This that had happened could not be spoken about, for I knew that in the describing I would have relegated it into the past. It would have become yet one more experience that had been labeled, and the very process of doing that would only take me out of the sweet stillness of the moment I was in.

Grace is like this. We cannot drag any previous thoughts, ideas, or experiences into this moment and use them as devices for comparison, since dragging in anything from the past obscures the grace and beauty of the moment that is here now.

It is only when, unguardedly, *all expectation is left out of the picture*, and all awareness falls on the now, that bliss, reverence, and gratitude become the natural expressions of the heart. It's when there is no movement to even *think* of the future, nor any desire to reexperience the past, that all grace is here, all bliss is available, all reverence flows through.

In unguarded innocence, reverence is the natural expression of the heart.

One sunset is not better than the next. In fact, it isn't the sunset that creates bliss at all, for it is not what is seen but *who is seeing* that makes the difference. The grace within you sees just this moment and is awed at its own creation.

✦

WHEN WE ARE FULLY PRESENT, open to all creation, with no thought of either past or future, content with just this, all reverence arises as a natural expression of grace.

And when reverence arises, another fragrance of grace seems to accompany it: honoring. As soon as gratitude or appreciation for creation is here, a natural desire to honor, cherish, and care for the beauty arises alongside it. It's as if they are two wings of the same bird. Reverence always inspires honoring, and when you honor and care for something deeply, reverence deepens. Reverence and honoring go hand in hand.

Here is another story that is one of my personal favorites, as it pulls you into the power of honoring and leaves you lost in simple gratitude and reverence. So, once again, you might like to settle in, relax, and open to let this beautiful story do its work.

✦

THERE ONCE WAS A WOMAN who had grown very sloppy in her ways. She had gained weight, was feeling a secret, barely perceptible self-loathing, and had fallen into a mild depression. Without her noticing, her external environment had begun to reflect her internal dishevelment and dishonoring. She felt heavier, and she really didn't have the energy to pick up the growing clutter that was increasingly piling up around her. Magazines were stacked high around chairs, and the telephone book lay open with maps and handwritten notes crumpled behind the sofa. Books never seemed to find their way back onto the shelves, and partially read newspapers were strewn everywhere. Unfinished containers of takeout food had left crumbs and stains all over the living room furniture, and old television guides littered the coffee table and covered the phone — which didn't work because the battery was dead, though it didn't ever ring much anyway.

There was no space to walk or even place a dish *anywhere*. When she wanted to sit and eat while idly flipping through the cable shopping channels, she would have to push aside the previous day's leftovers so she could put her latest takeout containers down.

Her kitchen was piled high with dirty dishes, but she figured, "What's one more dish?" as she added another to the pile. The trash had grown too high for the bin and spilled over, but emptying everything into a large garbage bag seemed too much of a hassle. When flies began to buzz around the kitchen, she kept the window open, hoping the breeze would carry them away.

In her bedroom, her dirty, worn clothes were dropped wherever convenient, and some lay on the bed. But as she felt more and more tired, when she went to bed each night, she just pushed them to one side, creating only a small space for herself.

Upon rising, it all looked so overwhelming, and as there wasn't a clean outfit anywhere, she decided not to change out of the clothes she had slept in. Fed up with the mess, she settled into the living room with her coffee, which she'd poured into a paper cup — easier than cleaning a glass or mug — and began to peruse yesterday's newspaper.

As she paged through it, she quickly grew bored. She'd already scoured it for the more interesting bits, and she wanted to read something new, something fresh. It occurred to her that today's newspaper was likely outside her door, but when she contemplated the effort it would take to find her slippers, unearth her dressing gown, and surreptitiously scramble over the front lawn to get it before the neighbors saw her state of disarray, she got weary at the mere thought of it. So with dissatisfaction she turned back to the stale newspaper to look for any editorials or articles she might have missed.

It was while she was in this quandary of whether to get up or stay put that the doorbell rang. She looked at the clock on the mantle: it was 11:32 A.M. Who could be calling unexpectedly at this hour?

The doorbell rang again. Grudgingly, she went to her bedroom, found her bathrobe under a pile of clothes, and made her way to the front door, where the person was now knocking quietly, perhaps thinking that the doorbell must not be working.

"All right, all right. I'm coming," she thought with exasperation. "Like all I have to do all day is answer the door," she grumbled.

When she opened the door, the bright morning sun dazzled her for a moment, and the stranger standing there, shadowed and silhouetted, was a bit hard to make out. In his hand he held a single white rose, and he spoke warmly, saying, "I brought this just for you," as he gently placed the rose into her hand. She looked down at the flower, puzzled and surprised, and a little bubble of gratitude arose from somewhere inside.

For a moment its beauty transfixed her. How long this moment lasted she did not know, but when she looked up to thank the kind stranger, he was nowhere to be seen. Stealing her way a little farther beyond the doorway, she peered in all directions, but there was no one in her quiet, sleepy street. It was as if the stranger had vanished into thin air.

Stunned and a little dazed by the light of the day and the experience of the unknown gentleman, she returned to the living room with her single white rose. Not seeing anything to put it in, she searched an unused back cupboard in the kitchen and found a small bud vase. She filled it with water, and was about to put her rose into it, when she noticed that the vase was dusty. Without thinking, she gave it a good clean rinse, clipped the bottom of the rose's stem, and put it into the vase.

She didn't notice it, but somehow she was walking with a little more energy in her step as she returned to the living room to find a place on the coffee table for her new present. She moved a few magazines onto the floor and created a clear spot right in the center of the table.

She sat down and took a moment to gaze intently at the flower so generously given her by someone she didn't even know. She noticed intricate details — the beauty of its petals, the greenness of its leaves, the texture and striations in the tightly held bud. She was surprised at its simplicity and at its remarkable beauty. It was, after all, merely a simple white rose. Yet something about it seemed special. It crept under her guard.

She opened her old newspaper — still not having ventured far enough outside to pick up a fresh one — but she soon put it down, so drawn was she to the beauty of her simple rose. As she admired it, she became aware of all the clutter surrounding it, and she thought, "This rose is too beautiful to be sullied by all this mess." She quickly cleared off the entire coffee table, taking the trash right out to the big garbage can in the back garden.

She sat down again to read her old newspaper, but found she still could not take her eyes off the beautiful rose. It was exquisite.

Rapt in its beauty, her eye fell on all the clutter *surrounding* the coffee table. "Oh my God. It's such a mess in here," she thought. "This rose doesn't deserve to be surrounded by this filth." With alacrity and a little disgust, the woman vigorously began to clear away all the rubble. She stacked the newspapers, organized the magazines, put the telephone book back in a drawer and the books back on the shelf.

"Ah," she sighed when she was done. "There's more breathing space in here. Now, my beautiful rose has a place to flourish and bloom."

The next morning, she got up as she usually did and entered the living room. She'd forgotten all about the rose... but then stopped in midstride. There it was: its petals blooming even more fully — it was absolutely stunning. For a moment she held her breath, so exquisite was this unexpected sight.

Then she noticed all the crumbs on the carpet and the stains on the upholstery and the grimy film on the windows.

They stood out like a sore thumb, in stark contrast to the pristine beauty of this immaculate rose.

"That rose is far too special to be surrounded by anything less than sparkling cleanliness," said the woman to herself. So she went straight to work, got out all her cleaning supplies, and polished her living room until it was shining from top to bottom. She spent the entire morning wiping, laundering, polishing, vacuuming, and dusting. She threw out all the trash and old newspapers, and she even rearranged the furniture, so that her exquisite rose would have plenty of room to breathe and expand in its beauty.

Finally, at four o'clock, she sat down to rest. She picked up a book she'd been meaning to read for months, but even as she opened it, the book fell slack in her hands. Quietly, she grew still — lost in reverence at the beauty before her. How could so much beauty be gifted to her? she wondered, as she basked in the glow of its radiance.

Sitting there mesmerized, she became aware of a putrid smell wafting in from the kitchen. The second she noticed it, she grew restless. She knew it would interfere with her enjoyment and appreciation of the rose. So she tore into the kitchen, and for the next several hours she cleaned, scraped, scrubbed, and disinfected it until it shone like sparkling crystal. She took out the trash, ran the dishwasher, polished the pots and pans to a high gloss — until the entire kitchen radiated shining cleanliness. By now it was midnight, so she took one last grateful glance at her beloved rose, turned off the lights, and fell into bed.

In the morning, she went to the kitchen to make her

coffee, and she was dazzled by the light. She'd forgotten what a sunny kitchen she had. And, just as she was about to step onto the newly clean floor, she noticed that the bottom of her feet were sticky. Not wanting to track muck across her sparkling kitchen, she went straight into the bathroom to have a shower.

"What a mess!" she thought, "Why have I never noticed my bathroom was this dirty before?" Like a thunderstorm, she swept through the bathroom until it too dazzled with light, and only then did she step into the shower and thoroughly scrub her own body — as if this was the shower of a lifetime. She scrubbed her skin until it was pink, shampooed her hair twice, and put on her most fragrant conditioner. Afterward, she sprayed herself with her freshest cologne and finally slipped on her robe.

It was no longer morning, but that didn't matter. She poured steaming hot coffee into her favorite mug and went to sit with her beloved rose. As she gazed contentedly, tears welled in her eyes. How did she ever get to be so lucky as to have such exquisite beauty gifted to her? The rose must be divine in some way, she thought. She innocently thanked the rose, and found herself falling to her knees in gratitude for such beauty. Reverence for life flooded her being: gratitude for just this.

Time passed. How much time she did not know, but the sun's rays began to cast long shadows in the room.

Eventually, she became aware that the old robe she was wearing felt somehow inappropriate. Everything was now so pristine, and it was not. Not wishing to disturb the rose with any stale energy, she thought, "I'll just pop this into the washing machine, and while I'm at it, I'll get my other whites and give them a wash, too."

She went to her bedroom and beheld a horror. Dirty clothes were strewn everywhere. It looked like a hurricane had come through. Disgusted and a little shocked that she had allowed herself to get this far out of hand, she hurriedly picked up every item. She washed load after load, and while she was doing this, she emptied her entire closet. "I'm sick of this outfit... I haven't worn this in years," she mumbled to herself. She stripped her wardrobe almost bare. "It's all going to charity. I don't need it — it's dead wood cluttering up the place."

She stripped the bed, washed and ironed the bedclothes, and finally, when all was tidied and put away, she vacuumed, scrubbed, and polished each surface.

By the time the bedroom was finished and sparkling, somehow it was midnight again. So she went to the living room, took one last grateful glance at her beautiful rose, and fell into her bed's sweet, clean, ironed white sheets. She slept deeply, soundly, without even dreaming.

The next morning, she awoke to a soft, warm glow suffusing the bedroom. Realizing she was up just in time to witness the sunrise — something she had not done since she was a kid — she lightly jumped out of bed and watched from the window. The dawn was spectacular. With a skip in her step she went to the kitchen, made her morning coffee, adding a touch of cinnamon just because she could, then sat down in the living room with her glorious rose.

The rose had come into full bloom. It was radiant, voluptuous, and splendid. Once again, she got down on her knees. She thanked the rose and asked if there was anything more she could do to honor its beauty. She was flooded with gratitude, not knowing how to thank such beauty for finding its way into her life.

She walked over to the window and opened it, allowing the cool morning air to bathe the rose in freshness, and then quietly, not wanting to make any noise that would create a single ripple in the exquisite, radiant stillness, she sat back down to stare in open adoration.

She finally felt relaxed to bask in the beauty — she could totally surrender to it, drown in it; nothing else could draw her attention away. It was just her and her rose. Such simplicity, such completeness, so sublime.

Time passed in just this way: the woman adoring her rose; the rose radiating beauty, embracing her and enfolding her in its fragrance; the woman basking in the embrace of sublime being.

The doorbell rang. The woman, stunned for a moment out of her reverie, innocently padded her way to the front door. She didn't notice that her feet barely touched the floor — so light had her step become.

She opened the door to find her next-door neighbor, looking concerned.

"Oh hello, Margaret. I'm sorry to bother you. I just wanted to check in to see if you were all right... There are three days' worth of newspapers on your front lawn, and as your car was still here, I didn't know what to think. I wanted to make sure you were okay."

"Oh, sorry to worry you," she replied. "Uh...I've just been rather busy. No, actually I'm fine. Would you like to come in for a cup of tea?"

The neighbor nodded and said, "That would be lovely." But her gaze was puzzled, and as she stepped through the door, she said: "Margaret, I can't help notice how shiny you are. You look absolutely radiant. I'm actually dazzled by your light. What *have* you done to yourself? You look beautiful."

Margaret was surprised by the compliment, which nevertheless seemed completely sincere. She hesitated, then stammered, "Oh, no, no, Karen — you must be mistaken. You must be sensing the beauty of this white rose I was recently given. It's so radiant, you must feel its presence, even from here. Come into my living room. You won't believe how exquisite it is."

Together, they stood and admired the rose, but Karen's gaze kept returning to Margaret. Finally, she said, "No, Margaret. *You* are mistaken. It's not the rose — it's *you*. Your light is making that rose look even more stunning, but it is pale in comparison to your radiance. You shine like the sun. This rose has become beautiful in your radiant presence."

Stunned, and not knowing what to say, Margaret went to the mirror in the hall. The face reflected there was one she'd never seen before — it radiated beauty; indeed, it shone like the sun.

In that moment, she realized the power of reverence. All she'd done was honor that rose, cherish it, care for it, make its life blessed. And in the process she too had become sacred. She too had been blessed. She too became radiant.

✦

WHEN YOU TRULY REVERE LIFE, you are prompted by the deepest part of you to honor it. In the humble honoring, you become honored. In your blessing, you become blessed. In your loving, you become love.

Honoring and reverence: two wings of the same bird. You can't have one without the other, and with them both you soar on the wings of grace.

Invitation: Honoring and Reverence

Is there some aspect of your life that you have been treating casually, letting it become stale or unused? Or have you let something atrophy through lack of care, perhaps even letting it fall into disrepair? What follows is not an eyes-closed meditation but an invitation to experience honor and reverence in action.

Start by examining the material things in your life. Go through your home with a fine-tooth comb: go into every closet, cabinet, and drawer and get rid of anything that you are not currently using and do not plan to use in the near future. If it is not trash, let it go to someone else who could make good use of it. Offer it to a friend, loved one, or charity organization. Clean every cupboard, closet, and storeroom — and leave only what you really, truly love, cherish, and use frequently. Be willing to be ruthless. Be honest and clear with yourself: if you're not sure about an item, let it go.

Next, do the same with your clothes. Anything that doesn't fit or is rarely worn needs to go. Those old Christmas or birthday presents you never liked in the first place — out they go. Those outfits you loved in the store, but hated as soon as you brought them home — sling them. Again, be ruthless.

Next, go through your bathroom medicine cabinets and shelves. Toothpaste tubes, squeezed out but not yet dumped — chuck them. Out-of-date prescriptions, perfumes that have gone stale, creams that are two years past their sell-by date — toss them.

Check your kitchen: Is there an extra set of dishes you don't really use? Do you have two versions of the same pan, and only use the newer one? What about old, cracked, or chipped mugs and cups? Keep only what you use or love, and give away the rest. Again, be willing to be ruthless.

Once you've cleared out all the extraneous clutter, go back to the items you *do* love. Do any need washing, repairing, dry cleaning, ironing, fixing, altering? How can you *really* honor them and make them shine?

Do whatever you can over the next week to completely restore every item, be it clothing, computers, vacuum cleaners, appliances, ornaments — be willing to invest the time to bring them into top condition. Make sure everything sparkles and radiates newness and care.

Then do the same with your house or apartment. Clean it until it shines. Clean carpets, furniture, windows, counters, drawers, and shelves — even closets and garages. Let your whole house shine from the inside out. Really honor it, respect it. Turn each item over and recognize the blessing it is in your life. Really honor that blessing.

In your honoring, a deep reverence may arise — a reverence for the beauty, the magnificence, the blessedness of all life.

Next, turn your attention to yourself: Is there some way you have been treating yourself casually — neglecting your health, skipping meals, avoiding exercise? Do you miss out on pampering yourself? Are you thoughtless in the way you groom or clothe yourself?

Start with a good shower, and as you soap yourself down, realize what a blessing it is that you have arms, legs, and a body with which to experience life. As you wash your hair, realize how fortunate you are to have good shampoo and conditioners. Realize that you deserve the finest.

Then, when you get ready to eat, ask yourself: If you were truly honoring yourself, what would you choose to put into your body? How would you exercise this beloved body, and if you were deeply honoring, how much time would you give yourself to meditate, contemplate, or be still? If you were dressing God for this occasion, how would you dress the divine self?

In honoring yourself, you might like to treat yourself to some fun — perhaps in nature — or some inspiring entertainment. Experience honoring and respecting yourself *fully*. It is a choice available in each moment.

Then, next week, or whenever it feels appropriate, you might like to take time to honor your relationships. Contemplate how blessed you are to have all the people you know in your life. *Do* something to actively honor each one. Take time to praise them, both inwardly and outwardly. You might like to make a list of all the qualities you admire or appreciate in them. Open yourself to how lucky you are to have other souls who care for you in your life, and lavish your partner or loved one and friends with great care. *Choose* to honor them, even if only for one night. Experience the gratitude that floods through when you actively honor and respect your loved ones.

Then, consciously choose to let this honoring and reverence

overflow into the rest of your life. *Take* time out to truly savor the moment and the tiny nuances of the present. Just *be* still, present in the moment, open to what *is*.

Honoring is a choice. And when you choose it, reverence follows in its wake. You realize the sacredness of what you are honoring. In that, you are humbled, awed. There is a huge power in honoring what is. One moment spent in honoring floods your being with gratitude. Then *you* feel honored, graced, filled with joy.

It is a self-sustaining cycle: The more you honor life, the more you feel graced. The more you are graced, the more reverence you feel. The more reverence you feel, the more deeply you open and the more completely you give yourself into honoring. And so it goes...

The beauty of it is that this is available in *every* moment. Even if you stop right now and spend a few minutes just to honor, cherish, and respect what is here, you will feel the murmuring of reverence bubbling up from within.

The choice is yours — and grace loves you so much that it makes that choice available in each and every moment.

Honoring and reverence —
the wings of grace.
With them you
soar blissfully in freedom.

✦

5. EMOTIONS

*If you open into the core of
any emotion, there you will find
the peace you are seeking.*

*Emotions are your greatest friends.
They are the gateway to your soul.*

When I arose this morning and felt a compelling pull to
write about emotions in the context of freedom, I
was quite surprised, but soon it became clear why our feelings had to be discussed when speaking about the boundless
presence of the infinite.

We so often have the misconception that our emotions
interfere with our experience of ultimate peace: that they are
the storm that distracts us from spacious calm. They *seem* to
limit our experience of freedom and obscure the boundless
field of grace, which by nature is vast, free, and emotionless.

There are so many false notions about emotions. Some

spiritual traditions teach the value of *transcending* emotions, as if they were the "bad guys" hindering our experience of the divine. They say that enlightenment is what happens when we have become *free* from our emotions, as if emotions were the captors that imprison us in the illusion of life.

But even if we aren't familiar with or trained in these spiritual traditions, we usually learn at an early age that there are "good" emotions and "bad" emotions. If we cry as a child, our parents are quick to shut those "bad" emotions down, saying, "Come on dear, dry your tears. It's time to go to school. Chin up…" Only "good" emotions are allowed. If we feel fearful, shameful, hurt, or angry, we are taught to cover it up, push through, and be strong. "Bad" feelings only make us appear a wimp to the rest of the world, and a sissy to those more strong than us.

Pretty soon, *any* strong emotion can cause an instantaneous shutdown and cover-up, as we quickly try to transmute it into something more comfortable to society. Even if we secretly sequester ourselves away, hiding in our bedrooms to allow ourselves a few private moments to experience an intense emotion, still we often try to talk ourselves out of it or diminish its importance, and maybe even feel ashamed of our "weakness."

And so in both our secular and spiritual worlds, emotions become an invitation to go to battle. The instant anything arises that we or society feel is too emotional, all our strategies to annihilate, deny, or transmute it arise: we fight, resist, and try to explain it away; we argue, project, blame others, and blame ourselves. Ultimately, we start to develop more long-term strategies for suppression. We take up smoking, drinking alcohol, overeating, senseless television watching, endless reading of just about anything — all in an effort to numb and put to sleep any and all so-called unacceptable emotions that might dare to raise their heads and try to destroy our peace, or rob us of our self-acceptance or the larger acceptance of society. Emotions become the culprits to be destroyed before they destroy us. It is almost as if some terrible devil called emotions lurks within each of our beings, and our job is to quell them, oust them, subdue them, get rid of them, push them back into the recesses of our consciousness — back into oblivion, where they belong.

Some spiritual traditions train you to repeat mantras or incantations anytime a "negative" emotion arises — to avoid its ill effects and keep your attention on the supreme. Other traditions ask aspirants to submit themselves to extreme austerities and self-deprivations — braving the elements, chastising the body, undergoing fasts — punishing their bodies as impure vessels that give rise to these "bad" emotions.

Some yogis meditate in caves for years, so they won't be required to engage in any activity that might cause emotion to arise: that way they aren't plagued by these "worldly demons." Even some Western religions demonize emotions: either in confessional booths or testimonials to congregations, one confesses the sin of experiencing unholy feelings or impure impulses. Then you provide further penance by performing a series of tasks, the difficulty of which is dictated by how bad your emotion or impulse was.

Nearly every spiritual tradition stresses the need to get rid of or conquer the natural expression of human feelings, and those rare beings who seem to have successfully purified themselves of their unholy emotions are celebrated as saints or holy ones.

Indeed, almost everywhere we look, in every context, it seems that society is conspiring to kill our emotions, to suppress our natural feelings. It seems nearly everyone agrees with the culturally conditioned belief that most emotions are bad and must be subdued at all costs.

It's no wonder we can't experience peace for any length of time. We are always on the battlefield, fighting wars against an internal enemy — one that won't give us any rest, for as soon as we quell one regiment, the next surge of emotion comes marching behind it, in an endless stream of never-ending waves. It's a battle we all fight, even though we know it's one we will never win.

For as long as we have breath in our bodies and have life in our being, emotions will come as a natural part of being human. It is as if we are fighting our very selves.

What a fruitless, endless battle it is. It's exhausting. It's as ineffective as standing on the shore and holding up a shield against a tidal wave. In fact, it is our very struggle *against* feeling that robs us of our peace and disturbs our well-being — not the "negative" emotion itself, but the struggle *against* it; not the feeling, but the ferocity of our will to kill it. When so much effort is wasted trying to resist the natural flow of life, there is not much life force left to experience the inherent joy of life.

Then, when the battle becomes too much, we collapse

into depression, into a place of numbness, where the acute pain of the fight cannot reach us. We seek counselors to help explain our way out of the war zone, or we ask doctors and psychiatrists to prescribe drugs to block out our intense feelings. Or we engage in pointless and mind-numbing activities to distract us from our feelings: We zone out watching vacuous television shows. We wash the car or vacuum the carpets when they're already clean. We gamble or take recreational drugs. We chatter and gossip endlessly about other people's problems — all in a game of emotional avoidance. Or we temporarily raise the white flag and plead for mercy: we turn to God and pray, seeking respite, or we go to an enlightened master and learn to meditate or to recite mantras. At best, these things provide only a short window of peace before the next battle begins.

It never occurs to us to drop the role of warrior and cease the battle altogether.

Maybe we just need a change of profession. Maybe we weren't cut out to be soldiers in battle, fighting against life. It's just that no one ever gave us another job opportunity — they didn't offer us an alternative choice. Upon birth, society simply said, "Oh, another warrior has arrived. Here, child, take up your armor and shield like a good little soldier. Life is a battlefield, and though you'll never win the war, your job is to fight the tide of emotions, no matter what. If you make some inroads, we'll give you a medal of honor. If you succumb to weakness, we'll ostracize you. It's an impossible job, but those are the rules. Keep up a brave face. Now march on, young one, march on."

But, what if you decided *not* to play the game of war? What if you finally said, "No, I don't want to be a marine. I never signed up for the army in the first place." What then? What if you gave up all resistance? What if you simply refused to fight?

What if, instead, you said, "Come one, come all. All of my emotions are welcome into the ocean of love that is always here"? What if, instead of a battlefield, you discovered that life is actually an infinite field — a field of trust, openness, love?

What if, in this infinite field, all the natural flow of life's feelings were free to come and go? What if you provided no resistance whatsoever to the natural flow of life? I wonder what would happen.

That which you resist persists.

Your resistance to emotion perpetuates the very thing you wish was not there. It's in the moment of true surrender, openness, and acceptance that your emotions feel so welcome that they easily come and just as easily go. Resistance keeps your emotions in play and creates only more of itself. Resistance begets resistance.

It's time to call off the fight and welcome your enemy with open arms. When you put down your weapons, lay down your shield of protection, and look this so-called enemy in the eyes, you will see yourself shining there — for there is no difference between you. There before you is the most human of human beings. You are looking into the eyes of a friend, and that friend is your self.

The invitation is to finally lay down your arms, dear one,

and welcome all of life with all your heart. Your old enemy will turn out to be your closest friend, and the only enemy still at large will be realized to be resistance itself.

The time has come to befriend your emotions. They are the gateway to your self.

Let's examine our emotions. Just what are they? Right now, allow a feeling to give rise to itself — any emotion. If you are really welcoming, you will discover that it arises quite easily.

But what is it? An emotion is actually just a simple sensation in the body. Some of these sensations are comfortable and pleasant, and some are uncomfortable, but they are all ultimately just a bunch of physical responses to chemicals flooding through the body. We can either resist the flood or welcome it and allow it to flow through.

If we choose to resist or suppress the feeling, it only gets driven deeper into our subconscious and comes up more intensely later. When we resist an emotion, hold it at bay, it merely waits in the wings for the chance to come back on stage to be fully experienced.

However, if we welcome it, the feeling is free to rise, be fully felt, and subside naturally. As long as we don't engage in any story about it or stir up any drama about it — as long as we just let it arise completely, purely, without examination or analysis — then it will simply be felt and dissolve back into consciousness. In this way it doesn't get driven anywhere or stored anywhere. The emotion feels so welcome, so free, that it just dissolves in the bath of love provided and doesn't bother to habitually revisit us. In freedom, the embrace of love provides no resistance, and emotions naturally ebb and flow like the tide.

Have you ever sat and watched an infant playing? It sits completely content, just resting in some sweet innocence of being. Then, some strong emotion will come flooding into its consciousness, and the child will experience it freely and openly — providing no resistance to it. Out of nowhere, for seemingly no reason, joy will come through, and the baby will laugh, gurgle, splutter, and giggle as the wave of cause-less happiness courses through consciousness. Then, in the next moment, discomfort may arise: the infant will screw up its face, pout, clench its fists, and pound against the rails of the playpen. When this too passes, once again the infant will just rest in open-eyed awareness. It may notice a mobile floating playfully above its head and get lost in complete wonder. Next, it may reach for something beyond its grasp, and it will cry inconsolably in abject frustration. Eventually, each emotion melts away, and once again the child is left in open presence.

The whole palette of human emotion dances through an infant's consciousness, but because it has not yet learned that it is *supposed to resist* emotions, it just innocently lets the natural feelings flood through. Ultimately, the child is un-touched by any of it. The emotion doesn't stick anywhere because there is no resistance to it. Like a spring tide, it rises fully, is felt in its totality, then subsides and recedes. The infant's essence, its being, isn't affected or changed in any way. It remains wide open and free.

Of course, the infant has parents, and before the infant

can even understand language, the parents embark on the huge project of "socialization": instructing the child in the way of the emotional warrior and how to suppress, subdue, narcotize, and deny the simple, natural feelings that come through consciousness.

I wonder what would happen if we provided *no* resistance? Would our essence be touched in any way by what came through it?

I often hear adults say, "I feel so disconnected from myself. I just can't seem to access the *real* me. I've read in books that there is a huge potential inside, but somehow it eludes me. I sense it's there; I just don't know how to get past the blocks inside. I don't know how to find it."

Of course they don't! They've lost sight of the infinite self, of their essence — they're out of touch with their own hearts because they've spent a lifetime on the battlefield, *denying* the feelings that are the natural expression of their own essence. When they deny that expression, they deny *themselves*. They lose touch with themselves, and they feel separate, bereft, alone, distanced, numb, and disconnected.

And yet, every time an emotion arises, it's presenting an open invitation to experience your self. It is offering a doorway to your own essence, a gateway to your soul.

Sometimes as adults we end up on an endless search to experience the divine, to find the truth of our own being, yet every time an emotion arises, we push it away. In so doing, we push away the opportunity to open into the infinite. Our prayer is being answered, but we ignore the response because it doesn't come in the expected form.

This that you have come to fear and therefore subdue is, in fact, a gateway to your soul.

✦

MANY YEARS AGO I had a huge, life-changing experience of this, which forever changed my relationship with emotions and ultimately provided an opening into the infinite that was so profound it gave birth to Journeywork — the original mind-body therapeutic healing work for which The Journey seminars have become known.

Up until that extraordinary moment, I hadn't realized that *every* emotion is a potential opening into your self. At best, I'd viewed emotions as a hassle to contend with. At worst, they were a huge obstacle to be cleared, released, and let go of. But never had I considered the possibility that they provided an entryway into my essence, a doorway into enlightenment.

I had not yet realized that emotions and enlightenment go hand in hand; until then, I'd believed the two worked against each other. But I've come to realize that every emotion is a gift. It's as if my own essence is reaching out with an open hand, inviting me to come home to my self. My emotions have become my best friends, and like any true friend, they carry me into the best part of myself, into the love and wisdom inside.

Feelings are a priceless gift, which cannot be ignored. They are your invitation to come home to your self.

I first discovered this when I was sitting with a group of about 150 seekers in *satsang* with an awakened teacher in the early 1990s.

It was the morning session, and after sitting in meditation for several minutes, bathing in stillness, we began the question-and-answer period. The stillness in the room was palpable, permeating everything, like we were soaking in an ocean of it. A middle-aged woman raised her hand and indicated that she had an urgent question regarding emotions.

Her voice was clearly agitated and upset: "I want to understand how you're supposed to feel all this peace when strong emotion is in the way. You know, I don't feel like all the rest of you... You all look so peaceful, so blissed out. I don't feel peace *at all*. I feel tormented. How am I supposed to feel all this so-called peace in the face of anguish?"

By the end of her speech, her voice dripped with anger and sarcasm — almost blaming the teacher for her state.

The teacher looked her deeply in the eyes and said, "Just don't move. Stay still... If you stay still and open right into the core of the emotion you are feeling, there you will find the peace you are seeking. Just stay still. Peace is here, waiting in the very center of your torment."

The woman seemed shocked and skeptical, and with searing cynicism she began to dispute the advice. The teacher remained completely at ease, politely waited until the woman had finished her sarcastic tirade, then with compassion simply repeated her previous instructions. She finished by saying, "Don't believe me. Try it out for yourself. *You* discover what remains when all anguish has been welcomed. *You* discover what is there when you don't move away from the emotion, but just open *into it*, surrender into it, relax in it. Find out what is in the core of it. Try it out for yourself. Make an experiment of it. *Just don't move.*"

The agitated woman eventually settled down. Everyone in the room remained patiently silent as she turned her focus inward, presumably to follow the instructions she had been given. Her face, which had been contorted in anguish, hatred, and projected blame, seemed to soften a little. Then out of nowhere a hurt expression fleeted across her face. For a brief moment, she looked completely vulnerable, like a newborn — totally open.

Then I saw fear flash through her eyes; a confused, inner scrambling seemed to be taking place. I heard the teacher softly purr, "Good...good. Just keep opening. Go right into the heart of it."

The woman looked up at the teacher for a moment, like she wanted to be saved from drowning, and appeared as if she might lose her grip. She looked terrified and out of control, as if she was trying to grab onto something and couldn't quite grasp it. Then, suddenly, her whole body relaxed and her face softened as relief poured through her. She began to breathe normally, easily, and a visible light began to radiate from what had been a hardened, harsh expression. Her face was now shining with beauty. She had an almost beatific expression.

I watched the whole incident in wonder. It was incomprehensible, but somehow in the core of her worst emotion, she'd clearly found peace. She looked like peace, radiated peace, and her whole body was soft and pliant, her being open.

It had happened so fast.

After what could have been no more than two or three minutes, but which seemed endless, she finally spoke — softly, incredulously: "I get it...I get it." She smiled, and tears poured down her cheeks. "What a drama I'd created! There's so much peace. It's so easy... The peace was here all along."

She chuckled at some private joke, then continued, "Why did I make such hard work of it? Now I must look like all the rest of you bliss ninnies." She laughed heartily at the irony of it. The teacher confirmed the truth of her comment, laughed, and the session turned to other topics.

When I saw the woman later in the morning session, she still looked radiant, shining like a cat that had secretly got the cream.

For the remainder of the morning satsang, I felt confused and nonplussed. The teacher had given instructions that were the exact *opposite* of what everyone else was telling us to do with our emotions. In the "real world," if you feel torment or anguish, doctors prescribe drugs so you don't have to feel it, and therapists endlessly analyze its meaning and significance trying to figure out how to get rid of it. If you consult NLP (Neuro-Linguistic Programming) practitioners, they try to re-frame you out of it, so that it doesn't feel so bad. If you work with spiritual counselors, they try to find out which past life contributed to it, helping you put it into a larger, less painful context. If you go to bodywork therapists, they try to help you release it, and if you attend emotional workshops, they want to help you cathart it. Psychiatrists have it labeled, categorized,

and attributed to some early childhood event; hypnothera-
pists try to take you back through time to find out its deeper
significance; and nutritionists attribute it to a chemical im-
balance and get you to change your diet. It seems that everyone has the same certain belief: it's *bad* to feel that way, so
let's *fix it*. And, even though each discipline has a different
way to try to fix it, each is convinced that fixing is the only way
to peace and wholeness.

But this enlightened teacher was giving an entirely different, radical teaching. She was suggesting, "No, no, *embrace* it,
welcome it, love it so much that you surrender into it. Go into
the core of it, relax in it, and there, in the very essence of your
worst emotions, you'll find peace." And I had seen with my
own eyes that this actually worked: this hard-seeming woman
had found peace and ease in the heart of her torment.

I began scrambling internally. Had everything I'd ever
learned been wrong? Had we all fallen into the same socially
driven hypnotic trance, where we'd come to accept that we
had to get rid of these bad emotions no matter what? Had
we all overlooked the obvious — that if we really faced our
emotions full-on, felt them wholeheartedly, opened into the
core of them, looked the tiger in the eye, and actually offered
ourselves completely into them — that peace would always
be discovered there? Could it be that strong emotions were,
in fact, *good* things? My being reeled. It didn't make sense.
Either the awakened teacher was out to lunch, or the whole
world was so unhealthily conditioned that it didn't know up
from down or in from out.

My *heart knew* that what I'd witnessed was authentic,

real, true, but my mind was careening at the very thought that peace, or anything like it, could be found in the heart of our *worst* emotions. It didn't make sense ... but there it was. Finally, I decided I simply couldn't take it at face value. I had to try it for myself. A few days after the satsang, I decided I would go into silent retreat on my own and try the same experiment on myself. I simply had to find out if the whole world had gone mad or if in fact emotions were our key to enlightenment. I had to know it directly, as my own experience, not as some casual observation of someone else's realization. The fact was, it wasn't true unless it was true *for me*. And I simply had to find out the truth.

I told my husband about my plan: while he was away at work, I would take an at-home retreat to discover whether or not peace could truly be found in the core of my most feared emotion, the one I was most hooked by — because only then could I be certain that the technique really worked.

After he left, I cleaned the house, changed the message on the answering machine, turned off the phone, and sat down in a peach-colored chair in our living room. I sat there, holding onto the arms of the chair, not knowing what to expect. A sick foreboding feeling had been lurking in the background all day, as I prepared for the experiment, and now fear flooded my being. I didn't know if I had the courage to meet my worst emotion. It scared the dickens out of me. Tears flooded my eyes: I hadn't realized I would feel emotions this intensely.

I decided to meditate, to "calm myself down," but that made the fear come more strongly. It seemed unavoidable. Everywhere I looked, there it was.

Finally, I mustered all my resolve to face it, be still in it, open into it, surrender into it. I silently welcomed the fear.

For a moment I thought I might go insane with its ferocity, but I opened wider. If that woman in satsang could do it, so could I.

I gripped the chair as fear shook my being. I opened wider still and welcomed it, and just at the moment when I began to wonder if I could handle its intensity, something gave way inside. I let myself relax. My will caved in. I stopped resisting and just opened. I experienced a momentary relief and then, suddenly, loneliness. Sharp, abject loneliness was surrounding me. It was everywhere. It seemed impossibly strong, unbearable, but I'd made an agreement with myself that I would not move. I would stay open; I would welcome the emotion and go into the core, the very center of it. So I spoke out "Welcome," albeit not too convincingly, and the loneliness became more pervasive. It seemed like the whole room was lonely: the walls were lonely, the chairs were lonely, I was lonely... everything was lonely, and there was no escaping it.

Something inside of me was still resisting, wishing to get out of this place, but I heard myself say internally, "Relax, welcome, just be still in the face of the loneliness."

Unexpectedly, my being responded and I did relax. Somehow, I felt myself opening and falling into a millisecond of relief, then plunging into a pool of despair.

Now despair was everywhere. I felt hopeless, helpless, pointless, worthless, useless... abject despair. I'd never known such despair in my life. It was searing and all-consuming.

Part of me wanted out, to beg for mercy, but by then I

had realized that the only way out was in. I knew I had to say "Welcome" and mean it, even if it meant being swallowed up by despair. I had to relax and give myself into it. Resistance was still lurking somewhere in my being, but I breathed into the despair, relaxed completely, and let go.

For a moment I felt like I was dissolving, and then I became aware of being in the presence of something that seemed like a black hole, a vast field of nothingness.

Terror arose. What was this unknown empty field of nothingness? An inner scrambling began. The teacher hadn't said anything about a void, an emptiness. No one had mentioned anything like it.

A picture flashed of the woman in satsang when she looked like she wanted to be saved from drowning: she must have felt like I did.

Terror was everywhere. I was terrified of falling into the black hole, terrified of being swallowed up into some emptiness. I thought I might go insane in there, lose myself, possibly even die.

I held on for dear life. I resisted with my whole being. I summoned all my will. I couldn't possibly let myself slip into oblivion, just fall into nothingness. I might not exist if I went in there. Fear of dying flooded through. Fear of the unknown washed through. Fear of oblivion shook my being. I just couldn't surrender, not now — I might not exist!

I made my body rigid; I forced my mind into line. I kept repeating, "Hold on, hold on. Don't let go..."

And so I sat in my peach chair — absolutely stuck. *Stuck in resistance.*

I simply would not move.

After some time, the effort of resisting with all my might became exhausting. Sweat streamed down my back. I had resolved to really stick this process out, and nothing could make me leave it, but then again, no one had said anything about a black hole or a vast emptiness. Could this be a big mistake? Was this really supposed to be here?

I intensified my resolve not to give in or let go into the blackness, but I could feel my will beginning to wane. I could feel it softening, and I couldn't seem to muster up any more force to resist its pull to let go and relax.

I asked internally, "What if you were never to leave this place of hovering over the black hole? What if you were to remain here throughout eternity?" And something inside shifted. The possibility of remaining frozen in terror seemed even worse than facing whatever was in that black hole of oblivion. Something began to give way. I felt myself relax, ever so slightly. I loosened my grip, and then, whoosh! . . . like a soft breeze, I felt my resolve melt all at once. All resistance dissolved, all relaxation appeared, and as I let go into the blackness, I felt a peace softly pervading my being. As I relaxed even deeper, a lightness of being showed up and pure love flooded everything.

Everything became alive as a scintillating presence of love shining everywhere. The presence was inescapable; it saturated and permeated the atmosphere. It was in the walls, chairs, and carpets, in the air, in me, in everything.

As my awareness began to naturally expand, I realized that the same presence was in my village; it permeated the whole world, the entire universe. Inadvertently, I had dropped into a direct realization of freedom, of the infinite, and I realized it to be a presence that was everywhere, in everything.

It wasn't some passing state of meditation, or just a momentary experience of peace. This was the direct realization that who I was was shining in everything: that I was the very stuff that made up the fabric of the universe — an infinite, eternal field of enlightenment.

Since that day, the realization of who and what I am has never left me. Every part of my being knows that I am totally *free* and part of *everything*. And yet, the whole drama of life, all thoughts and emotions, continues to play out — it just happens in the vaster context of this wholeness, this presence.

My emotions were not some bad things to exorcise from my being. They were, in fact, the gateway to my soul and to the realization that my soul is shining in everything, everywhere.

Each and every emotion you feel is the divine reaching out to you, beckoning you to let go, fall in, and experience the boundless presence of freedom. The enlightenment you have been seeking is right here, in the very core of your worst emotions.

It's time to befriend your emotions, for they hold the key to the infinite. They are your route to your self.

It's time to come home.

✦

OVER THE YEARS SINCE THAT TIME, my emotions have become a never-ending source of self-discovery. I have now learned to open into them more easily; effortlessly breathing into any resistance; consciously opening, relaxing into the core of any emotion — and I have developed dozens of practical techniques for coaxing myself and others out of resistance. I use many of these at Journey seminars, and one of them is the basis for the introspection at the end of this chapter. The truth is that the moment you *choose* to relax into the core of any emotion, you drop through easily into the next, and open into the infinite.

Once you get the hang of it, consciously opening into your emotions, embracing them, effortlessly breathing into any resistance and relaxing into them, can become an easy process. At first it may take a little longer, since resistance to emotions is often such an ingrained habit, but once you get the hang of it, the whole process can happen in just a few minutes, and you'll find that opening into your emotions, embracing them, relaxing into them, becomes an easy process.

Children are amazing with Journeywork. They trust completely, and that is the key. They drop through their emotions into peace as effortlessly as milk being poured into brewed tea. There is no resistance or struggle for a young child.

It is only we adults who worship struggle. If something is easy or simple, we often consider it insignificant or insubstantial. We've created a whole paradigm called, "Create resistance so I have something to struggle with." Is this true for you? Do you evaluate your success by the effort it took?

Are you a ranking officer in the emotional army, struggling to win every battle over your emotions?

The time has come to stop the war, call off the resistance, and open your being into the infinite, the boundless love that is always here. Even after we commit to this opening, however, we can find the process is not always as cut-and-dried as it seems. In fact, we usually have a love-hate relationship with the same emotions we fight against. We fear certain emotions and are totally transfixed by them at the same time.

When we aren't subduing our difficult emotions, we love to feel them and explore their meaning. We hold onto them, recall them, even obsess about who's to blame for them, dramatize about how we've been victimized by them, gossip to our friends about how bad they are. We go to counselors to find out their origin, to workshops to bring them up and cathart them, and we entertain ourselves with endless mind talk about their significance in our lives. After all, who would we be without the drama of our emotions? They help make up our character, give us our color and our identity, don't they?

One of the things I've found to be absolutely true about emotions is that they are essentially fleeting. Emotions come and go at the drop of a hat. They can't last for more than a few moments, *unless* we give them meaning, create a story around them, and add our energy to them.

Without a story attached, emotions are just sensations that come and go. They have no more meaning than a bunch of chemicals flooding through the body. However, if we decide that they are significant, important, that they must be explored, analyzed, and understood — if we keep replaying the drama surrounding them, using our thoughts to enhance them — then we can keep emotions in play for as long as we want.

Emotions are just momentary sparks flickering in consciousness. However, if you pile on fuel, adding the lighter fluid of a little drama, feeding the flame with your thoughts, adding the newspaper of someone else's opinion, and if you then fan this now roaring fire with gossip or your therapist's opinion, you can really create a huge blazing bonfire out of them. Of course, the fire will eventually burn out, naturally, of its own accord, *unless* you keep adding more fuel to it.

The irony is that you are actually battling, fighting, subduing, and trying to oust emotions that *you* alone keep alive with your thoughts, dramas, and energy. Emotions require your concentration and belief in your drama, your story, in order to be kept alive.

What if you were to decide to stop the story...just drop it?

It's such a relief. Whenever a pure emotion arises, you can recognize it as your friend, welcome it with open arms, love it, relax in it, and ultimately, find freedom in the heart of it.

This isn't about "catharsis," which is a popular paradigm these days for ousting a "bad" emotion. I can understand *why* catharsis is enticing. After a good cry, or a temper tantrum, we actually feel some momentary relief — and that is intoxicating. But it still doesn't *solve* the problem because catharsis involves only "acting out" or dispelling the emotions, and inevitably those emotions come flooding again at another time. Only full acceptance of and complete surrender into your emotions will lead you into real peace.

So, what I recommend is no dispelling emotion, no acting it out, no analysis, and no collapsing into emotion either. Don't fight, struggle, or run from emotion — for eventually it will surely hunt you down and find you if you do. Rather, just turn and face the tiger directly, surrender fully, and discover the love that's in its core. All other avoidances will only prolong your pain. You cannot run from your emotions. If it's peace you seek, your only effective option is to dive into them.

Relaxing, embracing, surrendering, trusting — these are the only tools of a lover of truth. Turn from a warrior into a lover.

Emotions — they truly are your gateway to the infinite.

Guided Introspection: Emotions

Emotions are the entryway into the infinite. They are your route back to your self, and they provide an easy access to the peace that is already there, calling you into your very essence.

You might like to start by finding a quiet space where you can sit without interruption for as long as is necessary. This is not an introspection that can be experienced while reading: use the companion CD or record your own voice. Or consider having a friend read this to you so you can give yourself fully into your own internal process.

This introspection is designed to lead you into an emotion to find the peace already residing within it. The key is to relax totally, be open and welcome fully whatever shows up. If any stories or dramas or memories come up regarding the emotion, please do not entertain them or let them distract you — for all images are merely a way for the mind to pull your focus away from the pure experience of the emotion. They are simply distracters trying to draw your awareness into some mind game. Instead, let the memories or pictures go, as you notice the way they make you feel emotionally, and just stay open in the emotion…really welcome the feeling fully.

If a memory needs further attention and healing, you can always get a copy of The Journey and do a full Emotional Journey process to release the stored pain and come into full forgiveness and complete understanding. But, for now, with this simple process, just let any images come and go, and let your full awareness be in the emotion you are feeling.

If, at some point you feel like opening your eyes, there is no problem with stopping the guided introspection. All feelings can only last a few moments — they come and go as the natural ebb and flow of life. The vast, boundless presence that you are resting in remains untouched by the activity of emotions coming and going through it. No problem.

Just know that we are all in the baby step stage of learning to befriend, welcome, and feel our emotions, and each time you do this simple process, you will feel more and more relaxed, open, and easy.

It really is a process of learning to trust yourself. Over time, resistances will naturally melt away, as your being learns to trust you more and more.

You are a beautiful flower. It's time to open and let your exquisite magnificence shine. Emotions are your truest of friends. They are the gateway to your soul. They are part of the dance of enlightenment.

Begin with a prayer or intention that you long to learn to embrace your emotions — to welcome them, to say "yes" to them — and let your being know that everything is welcome to come up in this embrace. Even the hidden emotions, the tucked away and secret feelings, and the unaddressed and unfamiliar emotions are welcome. Even feelings you've never acknowledged — all are welcome to come up.

Then, sit quietly. Let your being settle, and let your awareness become vast and spacious...Let it expand boundlessly in front...spaciously behind...and openly and freely to all sides ...It is vast below...and skylike above...

Just rest in an open sky of presence.

Make your heart as wide as the world...wide enough to include not just *your* emotions, but *all* emotions that exist... even wide enough to include your ancestors' emotions...Really make the embrace of your love so wide that it can include all the suffering of humanity...Your love is that vast, and it is all-accepting, all-embracing, all-compassionate.

Now, specifically invite a personal emotion to give rise to itself within this embrace: really allow it to come up fully, innocently...with no need to change it, fix it, or analyze it...*Just welcome it.*

Let your awareness go to the place in your body where it seems to grab you most strongly...Notice the sensation of it as it arises in your body...

Now surround that area of tension with your acceptance, your own love...With your whole being, let the emotion know that you are open to really *feeling* the sensation of it...the full power of it...

If you feel any resistance showing up anywhere, welcome that, too — it's natural. It's what we've been conditioned to do. It's okay to feel even this, so bring your awareness to any resistance, and let it soften. You can let it know that it's safe to feel...The resistance does not need to protect you anymore...You are allowed to fully feel *whatever* is here...

Be kind to yourself... Opening into an emotion feels like the opening of a flower... You can't force it. You can only allow it — coax, welcome, and provide space for it to bloom into fullness.

Let your feeling be allowed to bloom... Let it become fuller still...

If an impulse to run away from the emotion arises, recognize it, acknowledge it... Know that this is natural... Bless it and surround it with your loving awareness... then once again bring your awareness back to the original feeling ... and allow it to be fully felt...

Our emotions can be quite timid at first... They are used to being shut down, stamped out, ignored, run from... Like rejected children, your feelings may not trust you at first... They may be shy with you... because in the past you've so often turned away from them...

Now is your chance to turn toward your feeling... whatever it is... Welcome it with all your heart... You might apologize to it for having been so judgmental in the past... Really welcome it with every fiber of your being... Fully accept and embrace it... Good...

As the feeling grows stronger, just be curious to know what is there in the very heart of it... Feel yourself opening, relaxing, and surrendering right into the very core of the emotion...

You don't have to fix it, change it, or do anything... Just relax in the core of that emotion... Seek out any places that you may be resisting... soften them... and deeply relax...

What is there?... Good...

Now, with the innocence of a child, feel yourself surrounding, opening, welcoming this emotion... allowing it fully... like a flower coming into full bloom... And then, with tender curiosity, feel what is in the core, the very center of this new emotion...

Feel yourself growing vaster…opening totally…and falling into, dissolving in, opening further into the core of it…

Just relax there…What is here?…

(From time to time, with an emotion, you can ask what's behind it or beneath it.)

Continue opening in just this way: as if you were gently lifting back the petals of a flower and falling in naturally, effortlessly deeper.

At some point, a vast nothingness, or a black open field or void of emptiness may appear. This too is just another petal. Just ask what is in the core of it. Relax and open, and you will feel yourself dissolving through it as well.

Eventually, if your heart is open and your being relaxed and welcoming, you will find yourself basking, bathing, soaking in an ocean of peace, love, light, freedom: a boundless presence of grace will surround you and suffuse you.

Just rest in this as long as you like…And you may open your eyes when you are ready.

✦

$6.$ GRATITUDE

*Gratitude is the most immediate
and instantaneous way to
experience grace that I know of.*

*Grace simply cannot resist a grateful heart,
and the moment you bring your awareness
to what you are most grateful for,
grace appears.*

*Gratitude and grace,
like two lovers, they fall ever more deeply
in love with each other, until they are lost
in each other, inseparable.*

Gratitude is the most immediate and instantaneous way to experience grace that I know of.

It is said that gratitude magnetizes grace. Like a bee to honey, grace cannot resist a grateful heart, and the moment you bring your awareness to what you are most grateful for, blessed with, and appreciative of, grace immediately appears. I've begun to realize that they are inextricably linked.

Gratitude draws grace, and when you experience the presence of grace embracing you, it evokes more gratitude. Like two lovers, they fall ever more deeply in love, becoming lost in one another.

Ultimately, there is no difference between the two, for to feel grateful is to know grace, and to experience grace is to feel blessed and grateful. It seems one cannot go anywhere without the other; these two lovers are too infatuated to be separated.

Of all the fragrances of the infinite that have followed me through the writing of this book, gratitude has been constant. Frequently, tears well in my eyes as I realize how lucky I am to be used as a vehicle of grace in the writing. I am overwhelmed by the tenderness surrounding me, the wisdom that arises, the joy and effortlessness of grace. I feel so blessed to be in its constant presence. How can gratitude ever be enough to thank the ocean of grace?

Gratitude is available the instant you bring all your awareness to this moment and really open your being to experience what is here. Even the simple swirling of smoke rising from a candle can evoke gratitude. When you take a moment to *notice* what is around you, everything becomes a window into gratitude, an opening into grace — the beauty of the fabric of your chair, the grain of the wood on the table, the pristine clarity of your water glass, the variety of fragrances wafting through the open window, the angelic innocence in a baby's eyes, the joyful laughter of children playing in the distance, the mere fact of a roof over your head. Consider the food that nourishes your body and the padding footsteps of those beings who live with you and care for you — even consider the unseen, the unknown, the stillness. An open heart cannot help but overflow with gratitude for this boundless presence.

Just bring your awareness to this moment and open your heart, eyes, ears, and being to *what is* already here, surrounding and embracing you. Every single experience in your life is an opportunity to fall into gratitude.

In order for gratitude to be true and full, there must be a *total acceptance* of what is here in this moment — even if what appears in our lives isn't what we expected, wanted, or asked for. It's when we totally embrace and accept *what is*, without wishing to change it or fix it, that gratitude overflows and grace is experienced as everywhere. Gratitude is here when you open your heart to thank life for its blessedness, its beauty — for life itself.

✦

EARLIER, WHEN I DISCUSSED NONATTACHMENT, I mentioned the time my family's home burned down in a Malibu forest fire. This event led me to a powerful experience of nonattachment, but it also led to an even more intense and overwhelming experience of gratitude. It may seem unlikely, but it's how I felt. I didn't expect to look upon my burnt home with tears of gratitude, but they arose because of my total acceptance of what life presented, even though the outer circumstances might have seemed unfair and unacceptable.

It was the autumn of 1993, and I had taken a couple of weeks to help my friend Elaine with a television episode she was directing in New York City. One morning, someone came into the studio to announce that a catastrophic forest fire was currently sweeping across the Santa Monica Mountains, along the coast of Malibu. The fire was out of control; California was urgently calling neighboring states to send more firefighters; and the fire had already been declared a national disaster. He said that anyone who lived in the Los Angeles area should probably call to see if their home was in danger.

When I first heard the news, everything stopped for a moment. I held my breath and became keenly, sharply present, totally aware. I said nothing. Elaine suggested it might be a good idea if I excused myself and went into the greenroom to get more details from the news: "You need to find out if your house is in danger, Brandon."

I went to the greenroom and was transfixed by the television newscasts. Fanned by very high winds, the fire was blazing seventy feet high and spreading by miles every few minutes. It seemed impossible: I wasn't watching some disaster movie — this was *real* life. The flames were spreading along my familiar coastline. And these weren't any old houses burning to the ground — they were the homes of dear friends and loved ones, and they were being completely incinerated in a seemingly minuscule space of time.

The smoke was too thick for me to see what was happening on the coastal beach area where I lived, but my heart broke open for all those who had just lost their homes. Most

Malibu residents don't have home insurance, as it's too expensive. This coast is such a naturally volatile area that disaster insurance needs to cover violent storms, large waves and sea damage, earthquakes, and fires — and the cost is astronomical. So my friends weren't just materially bereft, they were left financially devastated.

The next morning I got the news. The flames had unexpectedly leapt over the Pacific Coast Highway, and the little cottage we rented had been consumed in a matter of minutes. It was the only property on the beach side of the highway to burn down.

Firefighters had done all they could to protect our home — stationing themselves around it and spraying the roof with water before the fire arrived — but it simply wasn't the will of grace. Once our home caught fire, it was impossible to quell. The cottage burnt down like so many matchsticks. Our car exploded in the aftermath, and nearly everything we owned and had gathered in our eighteen years of marriage and family life was gone. As with our friends, we had no insurance.

At forty years of age, I would be starting life at the beginning again, without as much as a set of dishes or a winter coat to wear.

My husband had also been working away from home during the fire. He picked me up at the airport, and we drove together up the Pacific Coast Highway. I felt a growing dread gnawing in my guts. Seeing the devastation up close was beyond anything I expected: so raw, so real — not some hazy image on a television screen. We were faced with the unavoidable horror of it. Every bush, tree, flower, and plant had been scorched, and what remained were pitch-black ashes and burning embers, still smoking — a black moonscape dotted with an occasional house, sitting alone, somehow miraculously spared, but surrounded by a bleak wasteland.

As I gazed at it all, I became aware that there must be some reason why some homes were totally untouched, without a single scorch mark, while others had been razed completely to the ground.

It was as if God's mysterious hand had reached in and totally spared this particular house or that specific building amid an otherwise charcoal-blackened desert. I couldn't begin to fathom this mystery, but I could sense grace running through it: it was so obvious, so unmistakeably apparent. The destruction didn't look random at all. What the reason was — why some homes had been entirely spared, garden and all, while their neighbors' houses had been totally devastated — I had no idea.

But the hand of grace was unmistakable.

As this quiet realization dawned, an increasingly sick feeling of foreboding welled up inside. Despite seeing the hand of grace at work, I feared having to face *our* devastated home, and this feeling in my belly grew stronger as our car got closer to our section of the coast.

My husband and I remained silent for the whole of the ride. We were left speechless with the breadth and depth of the devastation before us. As we came around the bend near our cottage, I summoned all courage and quietly braced myself, expecting the worst.

Silently, we pulled up into our driveway. My husband turned off the ignition. Neither of us spoke: we just sat there staring.

My awareness was wide open. I wanted to take it all in — to really see it, to face it directly. All of my being became fully present, sharp. I was keenly aware and riveted into the moment. What remained of our home was a steaming, hollowed-out façade, and beyond the blackened, burnt-out embers was a clear blue sky above the shimmering ocean. The pitch-black beams created a stark silhouette against this vivid cerulean vista.

There was something strangely beautiful about it. There was life, in all her magnificence: all devastation, all glory, side by side in one stunning, dazzling view.

Tears began to well up: tears of gratitude. Gratitude for the beauty of life, for the magnificence of creation, for the mystery, for not knowing anything — gratitude to be alive, to be allowed to experience just this moment. All gratitude flooded, and my heart burst wide open.

I turned to my husband and said, "It's amazing how much better you can see the ocean, now that there are no walls there." He smiled ironically, and nodded agreement. He too was lost in a moment of complete awe.

We'd dropped all expectation as to how our home was *supposed* to look, and we had somehow totally, completely, and utterly accepted that what was before us was simply what *was*. No wishing it was different, no efforting to change it, no asking, "Why me? Why this house? Why was *our* home the *only* one on the beach to burn down?" Nothing but pure acceptance.

And in all acceptance, gratitude arose naturally, of its own accord. And with gratitude, of course, grace quickly came flooding in behind it. I felt embraced in grace, suffused with it...and because of it, somehow, I was the luckiest person alive.

We began to pick through the rubble, digging here and there to see if we could find a memento, some piece of memorabilia — something that would serve as a memory of eighteen years of marriage. As I looked at the charred, melted appliances, broken pottery, smashed glassware, soaked, half-burnt books — everything began to fade into insignificance.

It was just *stuff.*

I became aware of a huge love embracing me, wholly untouched by the leave-taking of items. It was scintillating as a vast presence in everything. The accumulated material effects of family life were gone, but something essential remained — my *self.* Somehow, the love seemed even more apparent, more exposed, more expansive when all the trappings of life had fallen away.

It wasn't at all what I expected to feel. Yet, there it was, as plain as day. I wasn't doing a Pollyanna snow job trying to deny the truth of my real emotions, nor was I trying to reframe what was taking place and create a more positive frame of mind. The simple reality was that when I opened fully, in complete acceptance of what was there, I realized that I was no less whole — nothing had been subtracted or taken from the real, essential me.

All that remained was love. I felt an overwhelming gratitude for this love, gratitude for *being* love, gratitude for the love in my marriage, gratitude for life itself. This love could not be marred, lessened, or altered just because my stuff was gone.

At one point, I came across a dented, barely recognizable souvenir from a beautiful holiday, and for a moment I felt a sweet recollection of that time, then a gentle letting go. I realized that the item would never capture the joy we shared as a family, and that the memory would always be in my heart. I remember picking up a piece of jewelry, wondering if I could salvage it. It had both monetary and sentimental value, and I held out the hope that it could be fixed. But as I held it in my hand, it just grew heavy, empty. It was nothing more than a bit of matter: it seemed dead compared to the shimmering, alive grace I was resting in. After sifting through all the rubble, ultimately, the only real things that remained were love and gratitude.

Over the next year, part of my learning was to accept whatever grace offered, no matter what form it came in. Someone would give me their old sweatshirt, someone else an unused mattress that had been sitting in their garage. Some gave me their old spiritual texts, and others offered me a vase or their second set of dishes. Grace was hugely, beneficently generous. Part of my dharma was to accept with an open, grateful heart and with both hands. It was gratitude for life that prompted people to share their abundance with me. Our circumstances were a vehicle through which grace could express itself. In giving, everyone was graced; in offering, everyone was blessed.

The ebb and flow of gratitude and grace: two inseparable lovers who come to dance in the embrace of acceptance.

"MORE IS ADDED unto the one with gratitude."

A thankful heart is almost impossible to resist, and it naturally draws abundance to itself. I'd love for you to get a direct, visceral experience of this power. As you read through the following scenario, imagine that it is actually happening — what would it really feel like to experience this situation yourself?

So, take a few nice deep breaths, relax your awareness, and stay open as you read.

Imagine that you are living in a lovely seaside village, and the two houses on either side of you are put up for sale and purchased at the same time. Your two new neighbors move in during the same week, and you are eager and curious to get to know them. You give them a couple of weeks to settle in, waiting for an appropriate natural time to introduce yourself. One morning, you spot the neighbor on your left mowing the lawn, and you decide to seize the opportunity to say hello and welcome her to the neighborhood.

After exchanging polite greetings, you ask how she is getting on: How is she settling in? How does she like the area? What is her experience so far?

After a slight hesitation, the neighbor responds rather downheartedly: "Well, I moved here because I got a great job, my dream job, actually. I was really looking forward to getting to know the area. But, I have to admit, being from the city, I didn't realize it would be such a stretch to live in a smaller town.

"Don't get me wrong, the people here seem nice enough. It's just that it's not what I expected, I suppose. The neighbors across the way pointed my husband and me to some beautiful cliff walks, but I didn't have the heart to tell them that it doesn't really interest me. The air is certainly cleaner and healthier here, but I'm not really an outdoor person. I mean, mowing the lawn is not really my kind of thing. And I don't much like insects or even animals — like that dog across the street: it keeps bounding into our garden and ruining our flowers and it tries to lick me whenever I shoo it away. I guess I've never been much of a dog lover, and I feel totally invaded.

"To be honest, I'm not used to having such close contact with people. It's so personal. In the city everyone minds their own business, and we just get on with things. It's a nice enough place, this, and it's got great sea views, but I'm not into sailing or swimming, and it's kind of wasted on me. Now that I've bought the house, I'm stuck here. I know prices have gone up since we bought, and that it's already been a great investment, but I really think I've made a mistake coming here."

The conversation winds down. You politely excuse yourself and go back to your house.

Now check yourself. How are you genuinely feeling? Are you feeling somewhat flattened or drained? Check inside. Do you feel any generosity toward your new neighbor? Do you feel eager to help and support her? Do you feel drawn to her... or mildly repelled? Just check your being — is there some contraction here?

Now, the next day you see your other neighbor on the right in the garden, digging weeds in the flower bed. You introduce yourself and ask how she is getting along: How does she like the area?

Almost before you can finish your question, your neighbor excitedly says: "Oh, I'm so happy to meet you. I just *love* the area. I feel so blessed just to be here. You see, I come from the city, and though I'm more used to an anonymous life on the go, I really love the freedom I feel here. The sea air is so sweet, so refreshing, and I don't have to tell you how staggering the views are. And that neighbor's dog comes bounding into my garden and licks me every time he sees me — he's so friendly. I've never been much of an animal person, but he's won me over hands down.

"This probably seems stupid to you, but this is the first time I've actually got my hands dirty tilling soil. Can you believe it? I'm actually weeding and planting flowers. I didn't realize how rewarding that would be. And the neighbors are so friendly, so helpful. One couple suggested I take this cliff walk, which I did. My God, I'm not sure I've ever seen such beauty, especially on a rainy, bracing day. It blew me away. I can't wait for summer. I'm not really the nautical type, but I'd love to give sailing a try. The yachts look so amazing.

"I didn't really expect to have this response to this place. Coming from the city, I thought I'd be bored. But I've come to realize that the city seems dead compared to the aliveness of a seaside village. I really enjoy getting to know people personally — I don't feel so detached. It's like I'm part of a community. And this is all on top of having come here because I got offered my dream job with a great company, and increasing property values have already made my house a great investment. I work at the same place as that woman on the other side of you. Have you met her yet? I don't know how I came to be so lucky. I'm just so grateful. I feel so blessed."

You smile, conclude your conversation, and go back to your house.

Now, once again, stop and check yourself. How are you feeling toward this neighbor? Do you feel inspired, blessed, grateful to have met her? Is there a feeling of wanting to shower her with more of what she is so grateful for, or in some way give her support? Are you already thinking of other sights and areas in the vicinity to introduce her to? Are you feeling like you want to enhance her experience? Do you feel even more grateful to be living in this village yourself?

Take a moment to compare your responses. Both neighbors were genuinely polite to you. They both live in your seaside village, with the same views, with the same neighbors with the same dogs — yet their responses were very different. One came to you with a cup half-empty, whereas the other's cup was overflowing with humble gratitude. Which did you feel more drawn to?

When someone is grateful — isn't it true? — you want to give them more of what they are grateful for. Life cannot resist a grateful heart. And when we approach life with a cup half-full, instead of half-empty, life starts to shower us in abundance. A grateful heart tends to begat more of what it is grateful for — because gratitude is a magnet. When we focus on how blessed we are, we tend to draw more blessings to us.

In contrast, an ungrateful heart tends to spiral down into a sea of lack and scarcity, and soon all that's experienced is what is *not* there, what is missing. When we focus on lack, we create more of it.

It is a simple but extremely powerful principle. Be honest: How often do you choose to practice thankfulness? Gratitude is a choice: it's available to you every moment, and as soon as you thank life, you are flooded with a feeling of being blessed.

Why not take a moment right now to express your gratitude? If you are somewhere private, just speak *out loud* what you are thankful for. For example: "I'm thankful for the time and space to be with myself." Or, "I'm grateful for the innate wisdom I'm uncovering in myself. I'm grateful for the friends, family, and loved ones that are in my life." If you like, you can start with the small things, then just let the thanks flow. Just spend five or ten minutes speaking out loud, as if to life. What are *you* most grateful for?

Give it a whirl. Put the book down for a moment and just experience how graced you feel when you genuinely thank life. If your heart is open, and your gratitude real, you will be resting in an ocean of fullness, humility, and grace.

✦

I HAVE EXPERIENCED THIS PRINCIPLE at work many times in my life, in both large and small ways. Recently at lunch, my partner, Kevin, and I were sitting in a small beachside café in Byron Bay, Australia, when a large frilled lizard walked over to us, ostensibly begging for food. The people around us smiled fondly, as this is a common occurrence, and went back to their lunchtime conversation. The lizard came right up to my feet, and as I'm completely unused to seeing such a beautiful reptile close up, I indulged myself in taking some moments to admire its colorful striations, its thorny head, its bright, beady eyes, its scaly skin. I was thoroughly delighted by its friendliness and ease around people. The couple at the next table noticed my fascination, and a warm conversation opened between us.

The woman explained that she was a local, but worked full time in Brisbane, about two and a half hours away by car. She was a single mom, and though it was a long drive, she had really come to appreciate her hometown in a way she'd never done before. She expressed how delighted she was to have a job in information technology, which was her specialty area and not one for which there was much demand in a small place like Byron Bay. She worked long hours, but she said she loved that her seven-year-old son got to spend more time with his grandparents, and she shared how grateful she was that her parents lived close by and were able to care for him.

By the end of the conversation I felt so full, so blessed by her refreshing view of life. Her gratitude was genuine, humble, straightforward, and simply expressed. When she left the café, I turned to Kevin and said, "What was it about that conversation that was so remarkably inspiring?"

"Gratitude," he said. "Many single mothers would have been complaining about the long drive, griping about the long working hours, and sad to have to let their son spend so much time with his grandparents. But she felt genuinely blessed in all ways. She was totally grateful for her life."

This was clearly a woman who saw all life through the eyes of gratitude. For her, life was graced indeed.

Gratitude is a choice.

It is something you can live in and live *from* every day. And the moment you open your heart to how lucky, blessed, and graced you are, grace begins to shower you!

I recently had a very powerful experience of this, one that blew me wide open.

I was giving a weekend retreat called "Falling into Grace" at a beautiful spiritual center amid a glorious rolling green countryside. Throughout the weekend we had been clearing out veils, concepts, and limitations and opening ourselves into the boundless presence of grace that suffuses all our lives.

On the final morning, as we were getting ready to go out-side for a celebration lunch, I asked the group if they would be willing to take a few moments to honor the staff who worked at the retreat center. While the nonprofit foundation that ran the center had been paid to host the seminar, the people who served us our meals were paid only very mod-estly. They were really volunteers providing selfless service. They were serving truth, and we had all been blessed by their generosity and kindness. For a moment there was a hush in the hall as everyone took that in.

We had been served by fellow lovers of truth: their love and stillness permeated the food that they prepared for us and saturated the atmosphere of the entire center, and I felt a heart pull to thank them and offer them small gifts to express our gratitude. Everyone agreed they'd like to take the extra time out and truly thank them with all our hearts.

I invited the staff on stage, and to each, one by one, I began to express our gratitude. As I looked at their radiant, humble, shining faces and realized the immense offering they all had made in caring for us with so much love throughout the weekend, I became overwhelmed. The gratitude I felt was too great to hold, and I burst into tears. I found myself bowing deeply to each, with my hands over my heart in prayer position. I couldn't seem to bow low enough or find the words to truly express our thanks. Finally, I found my head on the ground, stammering, "How can we ever thank you enough for your love of truth, your stillness, your humility, your generosity? These gifts cannot begin to express the thankfulness in our hearts."

By the time it was over, and we had sung them the song "Magnificence," the whole room was sobbing a flood of tears. Our hearts were blown wide open. Spontaneously, everyone began to silently bow to each other in a huge outpouring of thanks.

At lunch afterward, it was as if we were sitting in an ocean of love, our hearts wide open, hushed humility everywhere. Midway through the meal, Kevin clinked his glass to speak, and asked if everyone would join us around the head table. He shared how recently we had held an auction to raise funds for the Journey Outreach program in South Africa.

In South Africa, in addition to the seminars we offer, we have a beautiful, free-of-charge outreach program, where our therapist volunteers go into schools, prisons, tribal communities, addict centers, AIDS orphanages, and youth groups, and offer Journeywork to all those children and adults who could otherwise never afford this kind of healing work and teaching. Kevin explained that recently our Outreach organization had been gifted a parcel of land, on which we could build a classroom, seminar hall, and offices, which would become a free-of-charge sanctuary open to those of all races, religions, or backgrounds.

South Africa is a nation thirsty for healing, forgiveness, and reconciliation, and its government has already blessed our training of schoolteachers in Journeywork. Volunteers were already pouring in to create and support our proposed center. Kevin explained that what we still needed were the funds to cover the main building materials and construction costs, or around $30,000. At the recent United Kingdom auction, we had raised over $3,000, and he said he hoped we might be able to raise some more at this retreat by auctioning a small personal item of mine, one of no significant monetary value.

Everyone's heart was already sweetly open, and we were all aware how much the South Africans needed this help, how many lives would be transformed, how many souls would be touched.

Kevin started the bidding at $100, and everyone breathed a sigh of relief when the opening bid was received. The bidding increased to $200, then $300, $500, and $700. Then the bid reached $1,000, and everyone fell silent. I was so overwhelmed at people's generosity of heart, and everyone was moved.

A man raised his hand and quietly said, "Two thousand." Again, silence; then, $2,500, $3,000, and $4,000. All was quiet as the bidding reached $5,000, $6,000, and $7,000, at which point the dam inside me broke, and my heart exploded in overwhelming gratitude and love. South Africa's dream for herself was becoming a reality.

Kevin also had tears in his eyes and didn't know if he had the courage to ask for a higher bid. Everyone was totally silent, with tears streaming.

A woman raised her hand, and almost in a whisper said, "Ten thousand."

Suddenly, everyone became aware that the Journey Outreach Center was no longer an idea — it was manifesting right before our eyes. Gratitude burst wide open, and suddenly everyone wanted to give. Kevin said he would find a couple of other items to offer, and everyone came forward to be part of the vision. In one great outpouring of offers, large and small, a total of over $50,000 was pledged for the center. The building was going to get built.

It happened in a heartbeat. A few minutes spent in open gratitude, and a building for healing manifested. This dream *had* to be realized. It was the will of grace, and we were all vehicles in service to South Africa's vision. Gratitude simply had to have an avenue in which to express itself.

You know what the curious thing was? We were all aware that this wasn't even *our* vision. We were simply helping South Africa realize her own vision for herself, and we were graced by simply being allowed to offer our help. We all felt impossibly blessed to have been part of this holy action. We were privileged to be allowed to participate, and gratitude was the gift, in and of itself.

Gratitude can make *anything* happen. It has the power to bring to fruition the most impossible-seeming visions. And it does so effortlessly, joyously, and humbly.

Gratitude and grace: they go hand in hand as two inseparable lovers.

✦

IN MY PERSONAL LIFE, not a day goes by that I don't take time to thank life for its bounty. This is not some rote, hollow daily practice. It's a natural expression of a grateful heart; I feel so lucky, so privileged, that I cannot help but express gratitude several times each day.

Recently, for the first time ever in my life and in my fiftieth year, Kevin and I *bought* a house. It's a modest three-bedroom bungalow with a flat roof, uneven floors, and a dated 1960s look. But every day when I wake up and walk into the living room, my heart is flooded with gratitude. This humble cottage is perched high on a cliff top, overlooking the sea in a tiny village in Wales. The garden was lovingly tended by the previous owner, and it has grown mature and glorious in that love. The property is surrounded by parkland that gently slopes down to the top of the cliffs, with the roaring surf beyond. Sheep graze in the meadows and roam freely through the village, and the air is fresh and sweet. The view from our living room and garden is so spectacular it takes my breath away; the stillness is so full you could cut it with a knife. This New Yorker is lulled to sleep at night by the sounds of ewes calling to their young lambs and the lambs answering back to their mothers. This may be one of the sweetest sounds on earth. And I sleep deeply, contentedly, in the embrace of gratitude that I feel to have such a healing and inspiring place in which to rest.

And do you know what? The expression of gratitude makes life so juicy, so redolent with flavor, so fulfilling, that life only gets fuller, richer, more graced, more bountiful.

When you see life through the eyes of gratitude, all of life becomes awash with grace. Everything begins scintillating with it.

And gratitude loves you so much that every moment is an invitation to experience the blessedness of life.

Invitation: Gratitude

Are there areas of your life that you have been taking for granted? Has life been showering you with grace, while you've been looking at a cup half-empty? It's time to realize that your cup is actually over-flowing.

Gratitude always draws grace to itself. This meditation is an invitation to give thanks to life for all that you've been given. Grace cannot refuse a grateful heart, and it will shower you in return. So, you might like to get a pen and some paper or take out a journal, and let's begin.

Just take a few moments to breathe and become still, and let your awareness go to all the ways you've been blessed in life:

how you're blessed to have a pen and paper; how you're graced to have people in your life who love you; how bountiful it is that you can afford to eat healthy, nourishing food. Just let your mind rest in the huge magnificence of grace that has manifested in your life.

When you feel that your cup is overflowing, take your pen and let that gratitude express itself on the page: as you do, keep asking yourself, "What am I most grateful for?" Let small things come up as well as big ones. Remember the beauty of nature, your clothes, laughter. Let gratitude pour itself onto the page, and keep writing until you have emptied it all out. Be willing to fill up a book.

Then rest, bask, soak in the humility of realizing just how lucky you are: regardless of your life's circumstances, grace is always present. Just rest in the open vastness that is experienced when the heart has been allowed to fully express its gratitude.

Gratitude begets more gratitude. You may like to keep your list handy, to refer to again and spark a continuous, endless outpouring of gratitude. Consider making a weekly or even daily practice of counting your blessings. Make a new list each time and add it to the ones before.

Once you start, you may never want to stop, for gratitude is such a juicy experience. And the good news is it's a choice that is available to you in each and every moment.

✦

7. LOVE

*...and the greatest of these
is love.*

The way of love is not a subtle argument
The door there is devastation
Birds make great sky circles of their freedom
How do they do it?
They fall
And falling
They are given wings.

— RUMI

It is true that the way of love is *not* a subtle argument. There
has to be a willingness to allow the heart to be broken open
a thousand times, and a thousand times more, for the vastness

of love demands *all* of you. We cannot hold *anything* back from love: there must be a willingness to offer all of ourselves into the fire — even if it breaks our hearts, even if we are devastated by the power and immensity of its beauty. There must be the willingness to allow love to ravage us. For it is in the offering of our complete selves into this love that we fall, and in the falling that we are given wings — and are free to soar on the wings of grace in the embrace of love.

There can be no half measures when it comes to love. Either you fall in completely or you flounder endlessly, grasping for something just out of reach, tasting only a small fraction of its immensity. Love simply requires all of you. It is not like you can say to love, "Oh, I'll give *this* much of myself, but no more." The part you hold back will have a life of its own; it will fester and keep you feeling separate from the vast ocean of the infinite. When we hold back, we deny ourselves the joyous blessing of plunging into the infinite and swimming in grace.

There is a beautiful song by Kirtana that expresses this realization so poetically, so poignantly:

My beloved's love
is like an ocean that will draw you in
You can sink or swim —
but I suggest you drown
And come without your clothes
She always knows when you've got clothes or fins
And if you come up for air
She's sure to spot you there

And pull you down
…She's so demanding
let it be said she'll ask for everything
And that little bit that's left
To which you cling —
She's gonna want that too.

Like Kirtana, I suggest you drown — for the only route
into love is to surrender completely. There must be the willingness to expose utterly all parts of yourself, including your
so-called shadow parts, those feelings or aspects of yourself
that you are not so proud of. There must be a willingness to
expose even the parts of yourself that are scared, greedy,
wanting, insecure, unworthy, angry, frightened, needy, jealous, raging — grace wants *all* of you in your entirety: good,
bad, and indifferent. To experience real love is to offer every
last bit of existence up to it.

Gurumayi says, "That which you offer turns to gold.
That which you hold back turns to coal." The parts we hold
back from grace wither and die away: sequestered from the
light, no life can permeate them.

Love requires absolutely everything.

For many of us, even contemplating complete opening
up is a terrifying prospect. Often, we haven't even exposed
the truth of our pain to *ourselves*, let alone offered it up to the
dazzling, magnifying light of love. And yet, to retreat from
exposure is to retreat from love.

Love and exposure go hand in hand. You cannot have one
without the other. Yet by exposing everything, by bringing

everything into its light, love is experienced to be surrounding, embracing, and infusing us completely.

✦

Last night, we held an informal, personal satsang at our home that revealed the truth and power of this. At it, a soft, radiant forty-year-old friend was sharing how much she was missing her mother, who had just left on a plane for England after a particularly beautiful, rich, and heart-opening six-week visit. Tears welled in her eyes and her voice broke as she shared her love for her mom, sweetly exposing her vulnerability to the rest of us.

We listened in hushed silence — we all felt gifted and opened by her tender exposure and the depth of her love. "I just miss her so much...," she said, her voice cracking and trailing off.

I quietly shared how awed I was by their closeness, by the depth of their love, and I admitted that many of us wished we felt that kind of heartbreaking love in our relationships with our mothers. This kind of love is very rare, yet even as the heart breaks wide open, if you let go into it totally, you discover that love simply opens the gates wider into itself, exposing more of itself.

I told her how lucky she is to be able to feel love so fully, so humanly — for true love is like this: it wants all of you, and breaks you wide open.

So many people, when they feel the immensity of love's

power, resist its force and close a part of themselves off, as if to protect themselves from its intensity. But when we shut down to love, separation from life begins and a dull numbness can result: numbness to emotions, numbness to all of life, and an inability to find one's way back into love.

This was not the case with this radiant woman. She was open to love and was right in the center of its heartbreaking pain. I suggested that all she could do was ask for *more* heartbreak, to turn it up, to open her entire being wider into it — for truly, the only way out of the pain is to go deeper into it. You have to be willing to say yes to heartbreak, to surrender totally and pray for more. For as you let go completely into it, with no holding back, *your heartbreak is realized to be love itself.* Like a river held back by a dam, when you let the dam break, the falling in is experienced as a rush of ecstasy as self merges into self.

When she had finished opening into the immensity of the heartbreak, her whole body relaxed, and she looked totally relieved and at ease — she was left *as* love. Instead of missing it, wishing for it, and pining for a personal mother/daughter love, she had opened into the full force of her emotion, and she was left as an ocean of love so large it was able to hold her relationship in its vaster context. She'd let the dam break and had opened into the infinite embrace of love itself.

I said how it would be a gift if we all experienced this heartbreaking love, for it is the very nature of love to break through all our barriers of resistance and open us into an ocean vaster than we could ever imagine.

One normally quiet man began to turn red in the face as

an energy built up inside. "I never knew that love was this immense," he blurted out. "I've always held myself back from experiencing it because it seemed too large to hold. I thought I would get hurt, that somehow it was bad to feel this intensity of feeling. I hadn't realized that love can be so heartbreaking, and I've held my love back from each of you in this room because I've felt afraid of its force."

Then his voice cracked, his face turned bright red, and something exploded inside. A flood of tears poured out as he sobbed: "It's just so huge...this love. I never knew I'm so big. I've been playing at keeping myself so small. I was just afraid of the heartbreak...It really is a heartbreaking love." After a minute, he added, "I feel so much gratitude for this love."

To experience true love, we must be willing to have our hearts broken by it a thousand times, for in the letting go the heartbreak becomes love. Then love is realized to be not a personal love, but an omnipresent field of love that permeates all of life. Its embrace is never-ending, infinite, and complete. In this love you rest as total completion, utter peace, soaring freedom.

You are love itself.

The time has come to surrender completely. There is no escaping love — for it is *everywhere*.

✦

THERE IS ANOTHER REQUIREMENT OF LOVE. Not only does it want all of you in complete surrender, but it arises when you expose everything to your*self*. When you are willing to shine the light of love onto the parts of yourself that you are not proud of — onto the unaccepted parts, the unloved parts, the unwanted emotions, into all the darkened corners of your soul — then love will suffuse them, embrace them, permeate them, until you are left as nothing but love itself.

These parts of ourselves — like shy, frightened, unwanted children — deserve to be welcomed into the light. They need to be in order to experience true freedom.

To experience infinite love there must first be self-love, and that means welcoming every part of yourself into the open, into *total* acceptance. Only then will healing touch every aspect of our lives. Everything is welcome in love. Love is not picky or choosy — it loves absolutely everything.

On the final morning of a recent retreat, a beautiful New Zealand man named Alistair stood on stage to celebrate his fiftieth birthday by opening himself to the fullness of love. I instructed everyone in the room to share openly with him what qualities they saw in him, and I asked him to open and receive their praise. People began to call out what they saw: "I see strength." "I see vulnerability." "I see tenderness." "I see wisdom." People shouted from various corners of the room: "intensity," "kindness," "laserlike intelligence," "peace." The list went on and on.

Sitting next to him on the stage, I could sense that it was beginning to be too much for him to hold: he was subtly bracing himself, not allowing the words to fully penetrate, as if he couldn't quite allow in all the beauty that was being reflected back to him. His body, though open, was also stiff, as if he was afraid he might lose control or break if he really allowed the truth to reach inside him.

I whispered, "I suggest you drown. You can't hold back this tidal wave with some imagined shield. I suggest you surrender. Just drown in the love." And something broke — a chink cracked open and, in one moment, all his armor crumbled and fell away. Tears started streaming down his cheeks.

With no barriers to feeling, the room became an ocean of love — unbridled, unguarded love. Alistair sat in complete unguarded exposure for everyone to see, as we reflected back to him what was truly there.

"Ocean of love," someone said. "Innocence," said another. "All love," I said quietly. "All love."

And so it is: all love is here the moment complete and total exposure occurs.

Then I asked everyone if they'd like to experience this for themselves, and everyone paired up, facing each other.

I suggested everyone take down their imaginary armor and be willing to open into complete exposure. Each partner began by saying: "Thank you for your openness. I'm sure I have the same issues as you. You are my mirror, and it's such a privilege to sit here with you. Thank you for exposing *my* issues through your openness."

Then the first person asked the second: "What feelings have you been hiding from in yourself? What shy, hidden emotions haven't you wanted to expose? What are some of the secret fears that you are not proud of? What have you not even admitted to yourself, let alone shared with someone else? What have you never spoken out loud before?"

Everyone was instructed to ask these questions with great love and compassion, really welcoming complete exposure of the hidden, frightened parts. When their partner openly responded, they were to answer, "I forgive you. The universe forgives you. As part of everything that is, all forgiveness is here."

Then the person was to ask again, "What else are you ashamed of? What else have you been afraid to admit, even to yourself?"

Once again, as the partner responded fully, they replied with words of forgiveness: "I forgive you. All of life forgives you."

Each pair continued in this way until one partner was *completely* emptied out, washed clean, and all was forgiven. Then partners switched roles and did the same thing . . . emptying out all the shy bits, the parts they were ashamed of, the emotions they had never allowed themselves to feel, and the behaviors they had never been proud of. Once again, they too were offered complete, universal forgiveness and utter acceptance.

The room felt awash with love, as all the holding back was cleared out. All that remained was love itself. In the offering up to love of all the unloved bits, we were left as *all* love, all acceptance . . . total peace. Anything held back creates separation; anything you offer up to grace gets transmuted into love. *Self*-love leads you into the ocean of love. The river flows into the sea, and all the dead twigs it carried dissolve and become part of the ocean.

Invitation: Exposure and Acceptance

Why not find out for yourself the power of exposure and accept-ance? What follows is a guided process in which you can do just that. You will experience this most powerfully if you do it with another person, but make sure you choose someone you feel you can be completely open and honest with, and preferably one who will be willing to reciprocate and in turn be open and honest with you. If you don't have such a person, then do this privately, on your own; it can also be found on the companion CD (see page 221).

I recommend allowing at least fifteen to twenty minutes to complete the process, and make sure you are in a private and quiet place where you won't be interrupted.

You can begin by taking some deep breaths in and letting them out, allowing your awareness to rest on the breath, as your breathing slows down and your being settles.

Once you feel still, settled, and open, you can imagine taking off your imaginary armor. This armor has, in the past, shielded you from the full intensity of your emotions, prevented you from get-ting full access to them. You can let this happen now.

Once your armor is off, silently make a prayer, or put out a genuine intention to the universe that you are willing with all your heart to expose yourself to all the emotions you've been ashamed of, to all the unwanted feelings, the secret fears, the things you've done that you're not proud of.

Now open your heart…Make your heart as wide as the world — wide enough to include all these shy parts, all the timid, undeserving parts — and put out a welcome to everything. Just welcome up the emotions, the words, the secrets, and speak them out into the room. Let them have expression; let the totality of them be admitted, seen, heard, and released.

You can begin with words like, "What I'm not proud of is…," or "I've never been willing to admit that I feel…," or "I've always secretly felt…," or "I never wanted anyone to know this, but…" After each full emptying out, say the words, "I forgive myself. All forgiveness is here. Life forgives me." If you are working with a partner, he or she can say the words of forgiveness to you.

Continue emptying out and forgiving in just this way until you feel wide open, washed clean, and at peace. Take as long as you need. The important part is to voice these things *out loud*. You need to get them up and out. If you are alone, it might feel a bit awkward at first speaking out loud to a room, but eventually you'll feel how liberating it is to express the inexpressible, to allow up the unacceptable, and to free the hidden secrets. It's in speaking these things out loud that there is a genuine release.

Make certain that you always follow each emptying out with forgiveness: your self-forgiveness, God's forgiveness, life's forgiveness. In this way, you will feel as if your heart is wide open, and you are resting in an ocean of love.

Love and exposure: these are two friends that go hand in hand.

⋅✦⋅

LOVE IS AN EMBRACE THAT IS INFINITE. It not only suffuses all aspects of your*self* but it permeates all of life. Its embrace is the very fabric of the universe, and it cannot be subdivided into human-sized portions, for it is everywhere. Love is so huge it contains all of life.

Often we make the mistake of believing that the love we experience is attributable to one special person. In our hearts we mistakenly believe that this person is responsible for the love we are feeling, and instead of remaining wide open in the vaster embrace of the infinite, we contract our awareness down to that one person. We project our narrow band of love their way, personalizing the love, believing that the object of our affection is responsible for creating the feelings of in-loved-ness we are experiencing in that moment.

When we do this, we create separation, projection, and *need*, for if someone else is responsible for our blissful feelings, then without that person we are bereft, lost, and incomplete. So need arises, and soon we begin to mistake *need* for love, believing that it is natural to need someone — indeed, believing that the essential nature of love is need.

This colossal mistake creates much of the suffering in our lives. It's like we build a sandcastle of our love, and then invest all of our energy, life force, attention, and loving thoughts in this imaginary construct. But all sandcastles, no matter how well we construct them, are impermanent. In time someone inevitably tramples over them or the tide simply washes them away.

If you are truthful with yourself, you will realize that objectified love is merely a self-created, idealized illusion that you construct so that you can indulge in a little fantasy, fun, and make-believe. But ultimately, in the light of day, it is seen to be no more than a beautiful sand creation — which gave you pleasure for a short time while you gave yourself permission to believe in it. In itself it is not real love, nor can it ever be. Your love and happiness don't depend on someone else "out there." The sandcastle is an *expression of your joy*, not the *cause* of it, and the same is true for our projected, objectified love. They each have as much reality, substance, and durability as the other.

No one on the outside can create your love. Love simply *is*. And it is experienced when you open your whole being to it and expose yourself to the beauty of all of life.

Certainly, others are a reflection of this love, for they too are permeated with it. This is why, when you look at a young kitten, or a newborn baby, or a freshly bloomed crocus, love arises. These things don't *cause* love, but in our openness we recognize it, and love spontaneously washes through our consciousness.

What often happens is that when we feel opened, humbled, or awed by someone or something in life, we want to capture the moment, to somehow hold onto the experience. We assume the person or thing we were with was responsible for its arising, and they become the cherished one. We pray that in their presence the same feelings of exhilaration and bliss will come bubbling up from within again. It's as if Cupid's arrow has pierced our heart, and the first object we see we begin to dote on and crave. With this initial mistake, we begin to long to be with the "loved one," to spend more time in their presence, hoping to get the "hit" again. Then if we are with them and our emotional "fix" doesn't arise immediately, we feel somehow lost. Our object hasn't given us the longed-for result; it didn't satiate us and we still thirst.

Instead of recognizing that another person can't be

responsible for the way we feel, we turn up our expectations. The longing gets sharper, and the need for love grows more intense. We try to duplicate it, re-create it, capture it, make it happen again. But because we've collapsed our awareness and lost sight of the vaster embrace of infinite love, we feel even more empty and needy. No matter how long we are in the cherished person's presence, we *still* feel alone, separated. We crave an all-embracing love, but instead we become addicts, wanting, lusting, obsessing, waiting for our next fix, even though deep inside an inner knowing realizes it will never be enough to complete us. Very often, when we collapse our love and project it onto another person in this way, we feel separated from God, alone and forsaken, so we look to more and more people "out there" to fill the emptiness inside.

Our neediness then becomes a force that repels other people. For how can anyone else fill the empty hole inside us? How can anyone else shoulder the huge responsibility of being the catalyst for, and the impetus behind, our experience of love? Then, when our very need for love drives others away, we end up disillusioned, blaming, and resentful.

The time has come to stop believing in your fairy-tale romance. It's time to crush your illusory sandcastles. It's time to stop pretending you don't know who you are.

Married people sometimes refer to their spouse as "my other half." Whenever I hear that I cringe, for how can someone else complete you? And does it also imply that you are only half a person? We place a burden on the other when we make them responsible for filling our needs. Our neediness has nothing to do with them. All that has occurred is that we have lost sight of our infinite selves and begun seeking to find our connection through the other person.

In the past, I offered couples counseling, and I often came across couples where one partner felt repelled by the neediness and dependency of the other. The partner would confide, "No matter how much I say I love them, no matter how much I show them affection or spend time caring, it's like it's never enough. Nothing is ever going to fill their empty hole inside. It's a bottomless pit."

One man complained that he felt like he was just some inanimate object, used simply to fill the emptiness in his wife. She thought she was being attentive and loving toward him, but what he felt was her neediness drawing on him, not her love coming his way. He experienced her as having an unquenchable craving for attention that he couldn't fulfill. He said that, ultimately, her neediness was a turnoff — that her attempts to glean her sense of self and her feeling of wholeness from him were actually pushing him away and jeopardizing their marriage. He said, "It's such a shame, because I really do love her — I always have, but her neediness is driving us apart."

Neediness is a repelling force that has nothing to do with love.

The truth is, *no one else can make us complete. Nor can they give us the love we crave.* For love can neither be given nor received. It is an ocean to be experienced. It is an infinite embrace that you can joyously dance in with someone else, but ultimately no one can give it to you.

In your life right now, are there relationships that are based more on need than on love? Bring your awareness to a particularly important relationship in your life. Check your body. Be real with yourself. Are there ways in which you secretly, or even openly, feel that this person *gives* you the feeling of love? Do you believe you *give* them theirs?

What if there were some huge imaginary umbilical cord tying you unhealthily and codependently to this person? And what if you were to try an experiment right now?

Imagine that there is such an energetic tie connecting the two of you. And imagine that a loving angel is going to take some divine scissors and cut that tie. When this cord is severed, imagine that a huge, all-embracing love channels back through it and suffuses and embraces your loved one. Then imagine that this same infinite, all-embracing love comes flooding down your half of the cord, suffusing and embracing you with this love.

What if, instead of being collapsed into and codependent on each other's love, you danced lightly together in an infinite field of love — completely complete in your realization of it, and graced by being able to have a partner to flow through life with you?

What if you just delighted in your partner's presence and felt blessed by not being needed? What if you felt completely, utterly free, and lucky to share life with your partner, all the while fully acknowledging they *can't give you anything* other than to point you deeper into your own experience of love?

And what if you required *nothing* of this other person? And what if they required *nothing* of you? Instead, what if in

all freedom you chose to dance the dance of life together —
blessed in the joy of each other's good company, privileged to
be allowed to have a partner to celebrate life with in the
embrace of love.

What if the embrace was so completely complete that, if
that partner was taken away by life's circumstances, you discovered your wholeness would be no less whole, the vastness
no less vast? And what if, in all relationships in life, you held
all people in this lighter, vaster context? I wonder how joyous
and blessed your relationships might become.

What if all of life appeared in this freer, lighter embrace?

.✦.

I REMEMBER ONE LAZY SUMMER'S AFTERNOON when I
was about twelve years old, my grandmother drew me into
her little breakfast nook to share some jasmine tea and have
a philosophical chat about the nature of love. I always felt
graced with Grandma's wisdom. I adored her with all my
heart, the way young children do, and I hung on her every
word, eager for them to penetrate deeply, so that I could hold
onto her pearls of wisdom for the rest of my life.

She confided in me that when she was newly married,
Grandpa had been fiercely jealous if she even so much as
looked at another man. Her eyes twinkled in ironic remem-
brance of those times: she had been quite a radical woman for
America in the late 1920s. To begin with, women weren't supposed to go to university at that time, let alone do postgrad-
uate work, and she'd earned a master's degree in philosophy

and religion. She'd been a suffragette, fighting for women's rights, and she recalled how she'd dressed in the risqué styles of the flappers and how she'd dared to go without a bra. She'd worn hemlines that, for those days, went past rebellious, and she'd actually bandaged her chest to make it look mashed and fashionably flat.

"To your traditionally brought up grandfather, I must have seemed a real libertine," she chuckled to me, as she saw through the innocence of her own then-perceived recklessness. "It's not like we were wanton. We had plans to become missionaries in China, and we both had very strong spiritual beliefs, but of course we had to wait for Grandpa to get his PhD. And by then, war was brewing, and we were unable to follow our calling. We had been married over two years when the jealousy issue came to a head, and you know how much I adore your grandfather — I only have eyes for him." I knew this was true, for the pair seemed like two lovebirds, still madly, deeply in love even in their eighties.

"Well," she continued, "Grandpa used to fly into jealous rages, making scenes if I even had a conversation with a friend's husband. One night we were all at a dance together, and a friend's husband politely filled in one of the slots on my dance card. Well, Grandpa lost it. He packed me up in the Model T and drove me home in an enraged silence, and as soon as we came through the front door, he exploded.

"The next day, I sat him down and told him that if he ever treated me in that way again, I would leave him. Now, you know my dear, that would have broken my heart, but I wasn't willing to be suffocated by his jealousy. Jealousy and love have nothing to do with each other.

"Grandpa admitted to me that he was just a humble son of a farmer who had grown up as one of twelve brothers, and when he met me, he thought I was the most beautiful sight he had ever seen. He couldn't believe his lucky stars that this hick from the backwoods of Nebraska could possibly be attractive to someone as lovely as me. And, he thought, if *he* felt this way, surely *all* other men must suffer in silence as they looked at me!"

Grandma admitted she was deeply moved by Grandpa's adoration of her, and she laughed at the silliness of his jealousy: "It's not like I'm some stunning beauty, my dear. It's just that he was seeing me through the rose-colored filter of love. We were both madly in love with each other — it was love at first sight.

"But as much as I love your grandpa, and I love him so much that it still makes my heart skip, I won't be smothered by it, trapped by it, or made less in it — because that's not love. That is need, my dear, and there's a huge difference between love and need."

Innocently, I asked Grandma, "Well, how did you end up staying together? Did Grandpa stop getting jealous?"

She paused, and said, "Well, yes, dear...love demanded it. I insisted that his love for me be so great that he face his jealousy down and finish with it — that those were the only conditions upon which I would stay in the relationship. And he knew I meant it.

"I explained to Grandpa my philosophy on love — that you must love freely, with an open heart and an open hand. You must treat love as if it is a delicate bird that comes to delight you by sitting in the palm of your hand. You cannot close your fist, for you will smother and kill it with too tight a grasp.

"No, simply, love demands trust. You must set your bird free to soar, and if it doesn't come back, it was never yours. But if it returns to you, for as long as your hand remains open, it is yours forever. So, my dear, when you fall in love with your first beloved, remember to love with an open hand."

I've remembered my grandmother's words from that day on, but now I might change the ending to, "If the bird returns to you, then you are blessed by it for yet one more day — for nothing belongs to us. Nothing is owned by us."

Love is free to soar on the wings of freedom with no strings attached. You can't own love. You can only bask in it, rest in it, be graced and blessed in it. And people will come and go in it.

I remember so clearly, when my first marriage ended after twenty years, that I was absolutely aware, right through the entire leave-taking process, that there was an essential love that was utterly untouched. The embrace remained whole, complete, and free during both the coming and the going of that deeply devoted relationship.

So how do you love completely and still stay wide open in an ocean of love, dancing freely in its embrace with your partner? I can't say that I've got it completely figured out, but I do know that I've fallen so deeply in love with this infinite embrace that I am not willing to contract into some narrow, tight idea of love just for one soul. I experience love as an all-embracing ocean.

I remember when I met my new partner and lover,

Kevin, I felt scared. I didn't want to sacrifice this omnipresent ocean of love for an ephemeral love that might come and go. I'm sure I must have seemed somewhat elusive, even fickle, in the early days of our relationship. In our intimate conversations I often spoke only of my love of truth, and I didn't bring personal, objectified love into it.

When I first sensed the delicate whispers of attraction, I immediately became hypervigilant: I didn't want anyone waltzing into my life and stealing this realization of universal love.

I feared that personal love would somehow take me away from the vast embrace of divine love. But these were unfounded fears born from my past concepts about what love is. Because nothing can steal *this* love from you: *this* love is who you are, and it is shining in everything.

Early in our relationship I kept Kevin at arm's length and approached the relationship softly, checking the waters to see if romantic love in any way obscured my experience of the vaster embrace. We carried on a long-distance love affair thousands of miles apart, with me in California and Kevin in the United Kingdom. In this way I was "safe" and could make certain that my love for a man would in no way interfere with my greater love of truth. At first, it was only a toe-dip. Then, weeks later, ankle deep; months later, knee deep. A year later, I took the full plunge.

Through the course of that year I learned that I could feel all kinds of powerful emotions and sensations: feelings of overwhelming attraction; chemicals of bliss in the body during a rush of arousal; deep appreciation and the feeling of being incredibly blessed; a surprising sensitivity and shyness; and a thrill of excitement like an out-of-control train. The whole emotional panoply of romantic love came to dance through consciousness, which delighted in the myriad ecstatic, trying, devastating, blissful, beautiful, soaring emotions that came through it. And still the sky remained whole, complete, no matter how big a storm came flooding across it.

Over the first year of our courtship I was the most truly human I've ever been, feeling raw, unguarded emotions without any protection — and through it all I remained identified with the vaster context in which everything was happening.

I survived, I passed the test. It was safe to love: to love wholeheartedly, with abandon, rambunctiously, totally, and turbulently. And I discovered that this "I," the essential love that I am, remained whole throughout it all.

To this day, Kevin and I still dance together lightly and deeply in this love. There is deep appreciation and daily gratitude; there are misunderstandings and out-and-out arguments. There is ecstasy, sublime lovemaking, out-of-control passion, gentleness, kindness, deep caring, huge mutual support — and ultimately, it is all taking place in the vaster embrace of *this* love.

Though we both work for The Journey in service to truth, *we face the same direction* — our joint focus is on freedom and service. Our vision is the same, and we both feel immensely privileged to be allowed to dance in this embrace, partnering each other as the one love.

Our schedules often take us to different parts of the world for weeks on end, but the completeness remains as we keep our awareness on the vaster context. Our greatest love is the love of truth, and our relationship is a gift from grace that allows us to dance fully in the vaster embrace, whether physically together or apart. And love is still teaching us both: we still feel like beginners learning our first lessons.

When truth is number one in your life, everything else falls into place behind it and in it, and all is graced by it. It seems that the deeper love opens into love, the more true and honest we must be with ourselves and with life. Love demands all exposure from us, and leaves us as an ocean of the infinite.

From time to time, attachment does arise for me. After being apart for awhile, some physical longing to be in the presence of my beloved mate still comes up. When this happens, I take time to choose to let go of the strings of attachment, and to open wider into the embrace, for I do not want any form of need to come into our love and sully it.

Sometimes when we come back together, shyness arises, and we have to open into a greater exposure and openly reveal our emotions to one another.

It's a constant learning, and the teaching is one that I'm sure I'll never fully get to the bottom of. For love is endless in its teaching, as well as in its embrace.

And you should feel free to let yourself love deeply and well: just leave need and attachment out of the picture. No ownership can abide in true love, for love cannot be won, earned, owned, or required. To love is to never fully know whether or not the other will be there in the next moment. To love is to surrender completely to this *moment*.

Love simply *is*.

Indeed, as Christ said, "...and the greatest of these is Love." That's Love with a capital *L* — it is a love that never ends. It is a love so great that it is here before you are born, remains throughout your life, and will still be here long after the passing of your physical form.

This is a Love worth making a marriage with.

✦

8. FORGIVENESS

*True forgiveness is one of the most healing,
releasing, and freeing gifts we give to ourselves.*

A life full of open forgiveness is a life of grace.

True forgiveness is one of the most healing, releasing, and freeing gifts we give to ourselves. A life full of open forgiveness is a life of grace.

Forgiveness is the natural, outward expression of the open acceptance that is intrinsic to freedom. The two are inseparable. In all acceptance, forgiveness arises, and when we forgive, we are bathed in all acceptance. And peace is the final result — peace on all levels of being.

I feel an overwhelming gratitude to life for teaching me the immense healing power of forgiveness. Forgiveness was the catalyst for my own healing journey, and all of the Journeywork now being taught around the world was born from the willingness of an open heart to release the pain of the past and forgive unconditionally. In Journey seminars, as with the exercises in this book, no matter how many processes we do — facing issues, releasing pain, recognizing ego's games, and so on — in the end, all our work comes to wholeness and completion with the simple act of forgiveness. Because it is in forgiveness that true healing begins. Healing in a very real way — physically, cellularly, in our relationships, with life, and most importantly with ourselves.

It could even be said that healing and forgiveness are synonymous.

I remember once reading in an enlightened master's book, "The root cause of all illness is lack of forgiveness." I would add to that, "And the beginning of all healing starts with forgiveness." If we lived in open acceptance and all forgiveness each and every moment, we would welcome life as it is with open arms, with no resistance. Withholding forgiveness is a form of resistance, and this creates friction and suppression, which can eventually open the door to a whole host of physical symptoms and problems.

Forgiveness is a route to freedom on all levels of being.

To get a taste of what I'm saying, just try practicing an experiment right now. Think of an issue that you haven't really come to terms with, something you regret saying, or perhaps some opportunity that has passed you by that you've never really forgiven yourself for not taking action on. Make it real. Find some mistake you made, something you blame yourself for, or some memory or aspect of your life that you've not forgiven yourself for, and, for now, surround it with a bath of acceptance. Take your time . . . Internally, say, "I forgive myself." Repeat the words and really mean it: "I forgive myself." Open into what it really feels like to deeply forgive yourself, and say out loud, "I forgive myself."

Now check how you're feeling. When I just did that exercise, I could feel some tears welling up behind my eyes, for the truth is I so needed to hear those words right now. And I felt a subtle release, a soft letting go into simplicity, into gratitude, into peace. What was your experience? Did you feel a gentle release or a soft letting go, and experience at least a brief moment of peace? If not, open your being wider and try it again, as these feelings almost always accompany a true expression of forgiveness.

Forgiveness can be one of the simplest, most powerful acts of release we experience in life. And the results reverberate not only through our own beings but to all those concerned.

And you can't fake it. This is one thing I've learned through Journeywork. You can't just repeat the words, paying lip service to the idea of forgiveness. It has to come from an open heart. It has to be real. Otherwise it is pointless; it simply glosses over the issue. In order to truly forgive, you must be willing to *open* your heart and face and release the pain there.

Real forgiveness requires humility. It is by nature a humbling experience. Forgiveness requires us to give up our righteous indignation, get off our soapbox, let go of blame, and let go of the pride of being right. It means we have to be willing to drop our victim story, soften our stance, and if necessary, let our hearts be broken wide open. If we can do this when we say, "I forgive you," a palpable presence of grace floods in instantly and we can tangibly feel the healing commence.

✦

THIS WAS A LESSON I LEARNED many years ago when, through grace, I healed naturally, without the use of drugs or surgery, from a very large uterine tumor. During that time I had a knowing that part of my healing would lay in uncovering old cell memories that were part of the co-creation of the tumor. I knew that if somehow I could unearth the stored pain and face and release the consciousness of it, somehow my body would go about its own process of healing.

I had read reams of research on cellular healing, and had seen dozens of case studies, and one fact stood out above all the rest: when we suppress a strong emotion, trauma, or painful memory — when it gets stuffed down, or tucked away, or swept under the carpet — chemicals are released in the body that can block certain cell receptors. This shutdown impairs the cells' natural ability to communicate with other cells in the body, and if the emotional issue, or "cell memory," remains unaddressed and stays stored in the cells, the cell receptors remain closed, and, in time, disease can occur in that part of the body.

I also knew that many of the people who had been successful at cellular healing had spontaneously gained access to these old memories, and when they released them, the body went about its own natural process of healing.

There was no doubt I understood the scientific principles behind cellular healing: I had read all the books available, and I recognized the truth behind the research — *but no one had given us a method to access the cell memories and clear them.* And you can understand all the science on the planet, and know all the statistics, but without a step-by-step process those case histories of spontaneous healing are nothing but a bunch of pretty words.

I was about three weeks into my own healing journey, and I was still lost and beginning to feel pretty sorry for myself. Obviously, I knew that part of my healing lay in uncovering these old cell memories, but I still didn't have a clue how to go about it — I didn't even know where to begin! I'd tried everything that I knew of, and I had to face the fact that I had not succeeded. The tumor was just as hard and just as large as ever.

Then one day I was getting a massage, and I clearly remember the moment a chink appeared in my armor of arrogance. I was lying there reflecting on my twenty years of experience and expertise in the alternative health field, and I had to admit, despite all the knowledge I'd attained, I had failed. In fact, when I inwardly admitted the real truth, I felt myself to be a complete and abject failure. I didn't even know what questions to ask anymore or where to turn.

Then something inside cracked, and I suddenly realized I didn't really know anything. I fell into a helpless, hopeless despair. Internally, something finally gave up.

I surrendered, and in that surrender I felt myself fall into the soft embrace of innocence. I fell into the unknown. I didn't *know* anything anymore. In that simple admission, something let go. I felt a palpable release. And spontaneously I opened into a bath of peace. I felt cradled in it and melted into it until there was no inside, no outside, just peace and a simple innocence everywhere. From this innocence I heard a humble prayer emerge, "Please let me be guided to uncover what's stored inside this tumor." As soon as it was spoken, my prayer was released into the unknown, and I lay there in the emptiness, not expecting anything, just being.

Then, suddenly and unexpectedly, I *was* guided. And when I uncovered the memory stored in the tumor, my arrogance instantly resurrected itself and loudly shouted in my head, "It can't be that memory — you *know* all about that old memory of violent abuse. You've been through all that. You are *so* finished with it."

But I couldn't afford to listen to my arrogant, know-it-all mind talk, so I opened my being and decided to really welcome the memory, to genuinely face and release all the pain that came with it. But in spite of the fresh opening and release, I still ended up in the same place of acceptance I'd been at for years.

I asked the peace in the room, "Am I complete?" The response was simple and clear, "*No.*" Again I fell into despair. Here I'd uncovered a so-called cell memory, but I didn't even know if it was the right one, plus I'd already dealt with it in the past! I felt helpless, confused, totally at a loss. Once again, something inside me just gave up. And once again, I fell into the soft innocence of not knowing anything, having no answers, not even knowing what to ask anymore.

As I did, I heard another prayer give birth to itself, "Please, somehow, let me be guided to completion — I don't know how to complete. I don't even know if this is the right memory, and even if it is, I've arrived at the same place of acceptance that I've been at for years. Please, show me how to complete."

There was silence. I didn't expect an answer. Time rested. Then spontaneously, unexpectedly, out of the emptiness a single word emerged: "Forgiveness."

Now of course my arrogant thinking mind raised its mouthy head and said, "Forgiveness? What a load of crap. Brandon, you've so long since accepted this whole issue; you've got it handled. You've done so much work on it — been there, done that, got the T-shirt. What difference can forgiveness make?"

But I thought, "You know what? I can't afford to listen to my negative thoughts. Besides, I have nothing to lose by forgiving, and possibly everything to gain."

So I gave it my best shot.

And during the process of forgiveness that followed, I realized *there is a quantum difference between acceptance and forgiveness.*

I had been at a place of acceptance for many years. That acceptance allowed me to carry a very self-justifying story around with me — how I'd been so-o-o noble, so-o-o compassionate, so-o-o understanding that I'd come to accept what had taken place. Kind, compassionate (arrogant!) Brandon.

To forgive totally, unconditionally, I had to open my heart, get off my soapbox, give up thirty years of my blame game, and completely and wholeheartedly forgive.

It hurt, because I had to face down my pride. I had become falsely noble, even saintly in my own eyes, and I had to own up to my own righteousness and finally give up the whole story — a story that had been a defining experience and expression of who I held myself to be. I had to give up my *attachment* to the story that I had been wronged by life. And when I finally forgave, when I truly opened my heart and completely forgave, the whole story of blame fell away and the consciousness connected with it was no more.

My story was over.

While I was forgiving, I realized that the tumor had never been clinging to me. *I'd* been clinging to it, and thirty years of dragging my victim story with me was finished in that one instant of pure, honest forgiveness.

The rest of the story is history, and three and a half weeks later I was diagnosed to be completely tumor free — no drugs, no surgery.

The healing power of forgiveness is palpably strong. It can heal bodies. It can heal lives. It can heal relationships. It can even heal entire nations. And it truly is *a gift you give yourself.*

✦

So often we make the mistake of believing we are forgiving the other person for *their* sake, but the truth is, whenever we forgive, we release the *consciousness* of the whole story that we've been holding onto and nursing, and when it's gone, we are the ones who are freed.

In my experience there are really three aspects to forgiving. First, there has to be a willingness to let go of our attachment to our story, to admit to and let go of our arrogance. We have to be willing to drop our self-righteousness and give up the "juiciness" we feel by being superior, right, or on higher moral ground.

Next, we need to empty out. We need to get real and recognize that behind the arrogance is the real pain and hurt we feel, and we need to open our being and let all the raw feelings that had previously been suppressed and unexpressed be fully felt. We need to release all the pent-up emotion, the words and the consciousness that were hiding behind our pseudo-armor of false nobility and blame. All of the genuine pain needs to be released.

Then third, once all the hurt has been met, expressed, and let go of, our hearts are open to uncovering the true learning inherent in the situation. We are open to experiencing what the other has gone through, and we may realize they were probably doing the best they could at that time within the confines of their own past conditioning, dramas, and pain. Once we've released our own pain, our heart feels a natural compassion and understanding of others' pain.

It's from that understanding and compassion that real forgiveness arises. It arises naturally, almost unavoidably, and it is completely unconditional. Once you've emptied out fully, forgiveness floods in to fill the void as a natural expression of grace. Forgiveness releases you completely from your story of pain and allows you to move forward in freedom in your life.

Indeed, forgiveness can become a route to freedom, if you are willing to drop your arrogance, open and release the stored pain, and allow natural compassion for others to arise.

In it all, humility is the key. For in true forgiveness, humility is always present.

✦

However, the second aspect of forgiveness described above is very potent and really needs highlighting. Over the years, I've experienced and witnessed thousands of Journey processes, and I've realized that for true healing to occur one *must* empty out all the stored pain, hurt, blame, and hatred. We cannot bypass the emptying out and releasing process and jump straight to genuine forgiveness, because the consciousness connected to the issues remains stored inside the body and it continues to have a life of its own. As I know from personal experience, that can be damaging.

Very often, people who are new to Journeywork think they can trick grace. They naively believe they can avoid facing their own issues, bypass feeling the true pain of past traumas, circumvent releasing the words and consciousness connected to them, and instead jump straight to forgiveness. They fool themselves into believing that healing will happen automatically once words of forgiveness have been spoken.

They believe they can gloss over their own pain by being Mr. Nice Guy or Ms. Nice Girl and offer "sincere" forgiveness. I call this pseudo-forgiveness. It just doesn't work. People often justify their attempts at pseudo-forgiveness by saying, "But I don't want to say anything mean or hurtful. I realize that person is not here right now, but I just don't want to put any bad thoughts out there."

I always answer like this: "The issue and its associated emotions are already stored inside your body. You can take forty-five minutes to humbly, honestly, and completely admit, face, and empty out all the stored pain, release the unexpressed emotions, clear the entire issue, and be finished with it for the rest of your life, or you can leak it out, hurting that person continually for the rest of their life.

"Those hateful, hurtful words are already present inside you. And you can finally admit them, release them, and be done with them once and for all, or you can harbor these thoughts inside you and let their destructive work be ongoing. I promise you the other person is already getting your strong nonverbal communication on a daily basis.

"And what do you think is more healing for you, facing and clearing it or holding onto it, stringing it out over time?"

Of course, once people see the true nature of the choice they are making, they always decide to pursue true forgiveness and real healing. Yes, there may be some intense feelings to be felt and some strong words that need to be voiced for a few moments, but that is far more healing than stuffing it back down and letting it leak out on a daily basis, eking out the underlying pain over the years.

For forgiveness to be truly effective and healing, *you* must be free and you *must* be true.

Guided Introspection: Emptying Out

Why not experience this for yourself? I recommend either using the companion CD (see page 221) or recording your voice and following along. You could have a friend read this to you if you can fully relax in their presence and give yourself openly to the process, which may take anywhere from thirty to forty-five minutes. You may each be more comfortable and trusting if you agree to take turns doing the process with each other. If you or a friend are reading this, remember to take sufficient time to pause when you are prompted to speak, allowing plenty of time to finish before moving on. Also, it's good to remember that you should speak out loud the things that need to be said, whether you are doing this process alone or with a friend.

Just find a comfortable position, and when you're ready, you can close your eyes.

First, bring all your awareness to this moment...Notice the sounds in the room...the feeling of your breath gently going in ...and going out...and just let your whole being settle.

Make your heart as wide as the world...wide enough to include all the acts of hurt, blame, and unforgiveness that have taken place in your life...Your love is so vast that you can even include all of humanity's unforgiveness.

Allow your awareness to expand spaciously in front...vastly behind...infinitely to all sides...and just rest now as a vast, open sky of all acceptance.

Into this sky welcome memories, people, and incidents that have taken place where you have felt unfairly treated, misjudged, hurt, trampled on, or betrayed... Really put out a prayer of welcome for any time you've felt unforgiving to arise in consciousness... All is welcome in this vast embrace.

If you'd like, you can also bring your awareness to your body and scan it... Notice any areas that seem a little tense, stressed, or contracted... Notice if any parts are hiding... If so, welcome them, too... Let your love, your full awareness, surround that area and simply ask, "If there were a feeling or words here, what would they be?" Just welcome whatever feeling is here... even if it's as quiet as a whisper... Just allow all the feeling to come flooding and ask, "When have I felt like this before?" Silently welcome any pictures or previous memories into your awareness... "When have I felt like this before?"

Or you can just call into consciousness a particular time when you've been the victim of unfair treatment or action — when you've felt hurt or judged by someone else.

When a memory, or a series of memories, has presented itself, allow yourself to imagine a beautiful campfire. The nature of this campfire is unconditional love, all acceptance.

To this campfire you can invite a younger you, age range from zero until now... Is the younger you there?... Good... Now invite the present-day you — the you who is here right now... Now invite a mentor of your own choosing — this person could be a sage, a saint, or an enlightened master, but it should be someone in whose divine wisdom you trust and in whose presence you feel safe... Are they all there?... Good.

Now it's time to invite the other person or people from the hurtful memory when you felt wronged or unfairly judged...

Is that person there?... Good.

It's time to let the younger you speak. The younger you has been through a lot of previously unexpressed pain, hurt, and upset, and now at last it is time to let it all up and out. Let the younger you speak openly about *how you really felt at that time.* Take however long you need to allow everything to come out — and know that the other person is protected by the acceptance and love at the fire. Let your words penetrate to that "deeper" place inside them, so they can hear what needs to be heard.

So, speaking from your past pain, what might the younger you say?...

When your younger you is finished, let the other person respond. Knowing that the other person was probably doing the best they could considering their past conditioning and internal resources at the time, what might they say if they were coming from the same deep place?...

When the person is finished, how would the younger you respond? What would you say?...

If the other person was able to really hear these words and responded not from ego, but from some place deeper, what might they say?...

Continue emptying out and conversing in this way until you both are completely empty...Take as much time as is necessary...

One last time, let the other person respond, and let your younger you have a last reply...

Now, if the present-day you could finally say what needs to be said, and if the other person could listen, what would the present-day you say?...Great.

And now let the other person respond...

And how would you respond to that?...

Continue emptying out and conversing in this way until you are both completely empty...Take as much time as is necessary...

And when both parties are completely emptied out, ask the

mentor if there is anything he or she might like to say about all this. What would your mentor say after witnessing this conversation?...

If you like, you can let the younger you step inside the body of the other person and really *feel* what they were feeling at the time...How were they feeling about themselves?...About life?...Go even deeper...How did they *really* feel? How did they secretly feel inside, about themselves and about life?...

Now step into their heart...into the very best part of them... Step into the part of them that they might not have had access to because they were feeling so bad or were shut down. This part exists in all of us, for in our core there is a great love, peace, and freedom. So step into their heart of hearts...

What is there?...

Now look out through their eyes at the younger you and feel how they were *really* feeling from their heart of hearts, from the level of their soul, at that time...

How were they feeling?...Can you see that their *behavior* was born from the pain they were in at the time, but in their heart of hearts they felt positive, even loving, toward you?

Now step outside this person and let the younger you open your chest and receive a lifetime of their acceptance. Let it fill every cell. Then *divorce* their actions, which were born from the pain of that time, from that love.

Now, if the other person could finally speak to the present-day you from their deepest place inside, what might they say?...

What would the present-day you reply?...

Let your conversation continue until both of you have completely emptied out and come to a full understanding...

When all at the campfire have completely emptied out, ask the younger you the following question: "Even if you in *no way* condone the behavior of the other person, and even if their behavior was totally unacceptable by society's standards and

there is absolutely *no way* to condone it, are you willing to completely and utterly forgive that person with all of your heart?"

If the younger you says yes, then let the younger you speak
that forgiveness out truthfully, in your own words...

Now, speak to the present-day you and ask, "Even if you in no
way condone the behavior, are you willing to completely and
utterly forgive the other person with all of your heart?"

If the present-day you says yes, then let the present-day you
forgive wholeheartedly, in your own words...

If by chance the present-day you says, "No, I can't forgive," it
simply means that you haven't emptied out completely, that
more release is needed. Just return to your conversation with the
other person and continue expressing your feelings. Express out
loud anything that you might be holding back, on any level, until
you have emptied out completely. When you feel completely
empty, ask your mentor, "What would need to happen in order to
forgive?" and then go ahead and let that take place here, at the
campfire. Then proceed with the forgiveness of the other person.

Now, ask if *you* need forgiveness from the other person for
anything? If so, go ahead and receive it...

When this is done, let all the other people at the campfire
merge into the light, sending your love and forgiveness and a
prayer that they find peace in their lives, so that only the younger
you and the present-day you remain.

Then let the present-day you turn to the younger you and
say: "I'm so sorry for all the previous pain. You just didn't have
access to all the wisdom that I do now. I promise you'll never
have to go through that previous pain again, because from now
on I will love and protect you."

And now, handing the younger you a balloon of self-love...
let the younger you breathe that in... Then a balloon of self-
acceptance... breathing that in... letting it suffuse your whole

body...Then a balloon of self-forgiveness...breathing that in... and letting it permeate you...Great...

Now hug the younger you and let the younger you merge inside, growing up now with all your beautiful internal resources, wisdom, and forgiveness. Feel them permeating your whole body.

Now you can let the campfire disappear, and you can begin to feel your awareness expanding again...becoming vast and open in front...free and expansive behind...infinite to all sides ...vast below...skylike above...And once again, just rest as an open sky of freedom.

And you'll find that you'll be able to open your eyes only as soon as all parts of you are fully integrated and ready to carry on this healing and forgiveness starting now. And when all parts of you *are* fully integrated, you'll find that you *will* be able to open your eyes now when you are ready, and experience the healing embrace of forgiveness in the room. Just rest in the freshness of the present moment.

❉

So how are you feeling? If you were innocent and real in your emptying out, when it came to forgiveness, it should have felt easy, obvious, almost choiceless, like it was the simplest and most natural thing to do.

Check your body right now. Can you feel the palpable sense of ease, relief, and peace?

When true forgiveness takes place, the effects are instantaneous, and they never miss the mark. It's a truth that cannot be denied. Forgiveness is a gift you give to yourself.

✦

Once you've done the campfire forgiveness process several times, there usually comes a time when the flashlight doesn't just point outward — it turns back in your direction.

In the beginning most of our forgiveness work is outer directed. We are letting go of all the past ways that we've been wronged by others, how we've been cheated by life, or even forsaken by God. So the blame is projected outward. And the forgiveness is of people or circumstances outside us. Then, over time, we run out of people and incidents to blame, and eventually life requires us to look at ourselves and see the things we've done that we're not so proud of. Life requires us to look at words we've said that we wish we could take back, and examine hurtful actions we've taken that we deeply regret. These campfires can be by far the most intense, but also the most profoundly healing.

Most of us are even harder on ourselves than we are on our loved ones. In a standard campfire process we may find ourselves quick to forgive others and let go, but harsh or even cruel when it comes to ourselves and self-forgiveness. We can have a tendency to be reluctant to let ourselves off the hook: it's as if we play God and judge. Yet for true healing we simply must forgive ourselves.

I really want to encourage you to do a few campfires like the one at the end of the Present-Moment Awareness chapter, and go through a full emptying-out session and a complete forgiveness process with yourself. The greatest healing of all comes from self-forgiveness. It's time to give yourself that gift.

You'll find that when you're able to forgive yourself, forgiving others flows easily, effortlessly, naturally. And living in a bath of acceptance and compassion becomes as natural as breathing.

✦

FINALLY, THERE IS AN INSIDIOUS KIND of unforgiveness that most of us aren't even aware of. We make internal, unvoiced vows that "we're never going to forgive so-and-so," and then we forget that we've made them, and the vows go on to have a life of their own. Can you remember how, as a child, when someone hurt you or called you names, you angrily shouted internally, "I'm never going to let that person hurt me again"? Or perhaps you promised, "No one is ever going to get to me!" Or, "I'm never going to let that person into my heart, ever!" And so on. Usually these vows begin with the words, "I'm never..." or "So-and-so is not going to..." Especially if we made them with some intensity of feeling, these vows can go on to have a life of their own, and they can be quite destructive. Then, as adults we don't understand why we're not letting our partner get close to us and can't feel deep intimacy; we don't understand why we seemingly have a wall up against life and can't feel the "juice," or why our heart feels boxed and hidden away and why we are unable to fully feel real love. It's often because we've made a vow that is perpetuating itself in consciousness, and it's rising as an impulse at an other-than-conscious level.

Such vows usually have some element of unforgiveness in them, and they can be seriously damaging to the relationship that you want to be open, intimate, and true in — and this can include the relationship you have with yourself.

So, I'd like to conclude this chapter on forgiveness by offering you the Changing Unhealthy Vows guided introspection. It helps you to recognize the unhealthy vows that have been made and gives you the chance to replace them with healthy, empowering, and freeing vows. And mainly it frees you from any unvoiced unforgiveness that may be going on at an other-than-conscious level.

Guided Introspection: Changing Unhealthy Vows

For this guided process I recommend using the companion CD (see page 221), recording yourself reading, or working with a friend. That way you'll be able to relax deeply and surrender fully to the process. It's not a process that you can do while reading. As with the Empty-ing Out guided introspection, if a friend is reading this to you, or if you are recording your own voice, it is important to take plenty of time to pause and allow the suggested images to arise and the visu-alizations to take place.

Find a comfortable position, and when you are ready, you may close your eyes...Take a nice deep breath in...and slowly let it out…And another long, deep breath in…and slowly let it out…Just relax and open your being…

And as you continue to relax and open…imagine that in front of you is a downward-facing staircase…And this shimmering staircase has five steps…These are magical steps, for they will lead you deeply into the light of your own being…into your essence…So, step now onto the top step, number five…

And relaxing in the knowledge that each step will effortlessly take you deeper into your own self…step down onto step four…opening down to three…deeper down to two…and before you step onto the final step, step one…let your awareness expand infinitely in front…and behind…Feel consciousness become boundless to each side…opening spaciously above… and deepening oceanlike beneath…Then step into the core of your own deepest awareness…as you step down onto step one now…And just rest at this awareness…

Now notice that to one side of you there is a doorway, and behind that doorway is the great light of your own soul…Also waiting here is a mentor…one in whose divinity and wisdom you can trust…So now, when you're ready, walk through the doorway, into the light…and greet your mentor…Thank him or her for being here to support you in changing an old vow that no longer supports you…

And now to the side is a very special vehicle…This is a time shuttle that will take you back to a time and place when a specific vow was made, a vow that has become inappropriate, unhealthy, or unsupportive to the person you are today…So you and your mentor can step right into the shuttle, take a seat, and fasten your seat belts…

Then look at the dashboard in front of you…Notice the blue button marked "old vow," knowing that when you press this button, the shuttle will take you safely and elegantly back in time...back to the time and the consciousness of that old vow...And either you or your mentor can press the blue button now...and let the shuttle take you where *it* knows to go...

And when you arrive at the scene, just allow the shuttle to come in for a soft, gentle landing...Great...Now you and your mentor can undo your seat belts and leave the shuttle, walking right into the scene where the old vow was made...You can also bring a guardian angel right here with you, if that feels helpful or appropriate...

Now take a moment to notice who else is here in the scene...And you can adjust the lighting level and the clarity of the scene until it's ideal.

So, who else is here?...Good...Thank you...Now allow a campfire to appear right here in this scene...knowing that this fire is the fire of unconditional love...of life itself...And bringing also to this campfire the presence of God, or the presence of the infinite or the universe...and ask either the younger you in the scene or the mentor: What unhealthy vow was made here?...What vow was made that is no longer appropriate or supportive in this life stream?...

Then, in the knowledge that God, the infinite, the universe understands fully why this vow was initially made, and that it is no longer appropriate to leave it in place..ask for blessings and assistance to undo and remove the old vow and to replace it with a new, healthy, wholesome vow...Great...

What old vow did you make?...What was the wording?... Thank you...

So now turn to the other people in this scene, and let them know what vow was previously made...and why it is no longer appropriate to have this old vow in place...Let them know that it is your intention to let go of the old vow and replace it with a new, healthy vow...Good...

Now go ahead and forgive those at the campfire for playing their part in the making of the old vow...And ask for forgiveness from God, the infinite, the universe for anything that needs forgiving...and allow forgiveness to come to you from all those at the campfire...

When this is complete, turn to your mentor and ask that the old vow be swept clean...completely cleared out from every cell of your being...Let the mentor sweep, wash, hose, vacuum away every vestige of that old vow...And you just watch and experience it as that old vow is cleared from every molecule of your being...from all of consciousness...Great...

And now ask the mentor to cut any ties or energetic cords that may attach you to the other people in this scene...Make sure that a beautiful light is sent through both ends of the ties as they are cut...Look into the faces of those who are being freed...Notice how grateful they are to be set free...

Now ask your mentor to help you formulate a new, healthy, appropriate vow...one that will empower you to be open, healthy, fulfilled, and free...free to be your true self...free to soar...

What is the new, healthy vow?...Great...Thank you...

Now ask your mentor to install this brand-new vow into every cell of your being...Ask the mentor to flood every particle of your being with this new, empowering vow...making it an integral part of you...revitalizing you...energizing you...letting you come to peace and completion...Take your time to allow this to take place fully...

When this is completely complete, send blessings to all those at the campfire...And in the knowledge that this new vow can only get stronger and more supportive over time...knowing that it will heal and guide perfectly and naturally of its own accord, without you having to do or think a thing...thank the other people in the scene for being here...Allow them to merge into the fire that is the source of all life...Only you, the younger you, and your mentor remain...Let the younger you hug and merge with the present-day you...letting the younger you grow up through all the intervening years with this new, empowering, healthy vow already in place...Sensing the changes in consciousness that take place as the old integrates with the new... right up to the present time...

When this is complete, turn to the mentor and ask if there is any more teaching to be learned here...Is there any insight or wisdom to be revealed?...And if there is, just let it be revealed now...Good...

And now that this is complete, you and your mentor can get back into the shuttle...And let the shuttle take you right back to the original doorway you first came through...When you've arrived, just get out and thank your mentor with all your heart for being here in support of this life-changing process of release and healing...Then step back through the doorway and walk over to the staircase you originally came down...

Now just step back up the steps:...one...coming back to the present time...two...feeling refreshed and renewed... three...stretching and becoming more aware of your body ...four...Pause here, and imagine stepping into the future a day from now...And feel how you feel a day from now, with this brand-new, empowering vow already a part of you...Great... And now step one week into the future...and see and hear and feel how it is to be the new you one week from now...Notice how differently you feel and how differently you are communicating with yourself and with others...Great...And now step into the future one month from now...and feel your being as it is flooded with the consciousness of the brand-new you one month from now...How is it to be the new, free you? How does it feel to be released, healed and whole?...Fabulous!...And now step six months into the future...and get a full sense of how your life is...how it is to have been free from that old, ancient vow for six months now...with the new, wholesome vow having done its work effortlessly for a full six months...So how does it feel to be free, to soar?...Great!

And knowing that time is just a concept...and that anything that appears in consciousness is already here...just allow the consciousness of the you six months from now to come back to the present moment...while standing on step four...Know that you will only be able to step up onto step five and open your eyes when all parts of you are fully integrated in the knowledge that this healing, this release, this freedom can only grow and integrate organically...perfectly naturally, of its own accord...

And when all parts are fully integrated and agreed, then you may step up onto step five...and you can open you eyes now, when you are ready...

Congratulations!...

✦

$\mathcal{9}.$ ENLIGHTENMENT

*The enlightenment you are seeking
is already embracing you, suffusing you.
It is shining as your self.*

*When all ideas and concepts about it fall away,
what remains is pure, unobscured awareness . . .
enlightenment itself.*

You are that.

While writing this book, I have known for some time that eventually this chapter would have to be written. With this knowing came an increasing reluctance to bring the topic onto the page, because I knew that as soon as the word "enlightenment" appeared, all kinds of notions would spring to mind.

"Enlightenment" is such a controversial word. Each and every spiritual aspirant or seeker seems to have a different, yet equally certain, idea of what they *think* it *should* be and what it should look like. Many people aspire to attain this ultimate state or to have a sustained experience of it, but no one can even agree on what it is!

The mind boggles with the myriad concepts and ideas that arise with the mere welcoming of this word into consciousness. Yet, welcome it we must.

Even in the simple reading of the word "enlightenment," you may already have had several images come to mind. Some might have imagined a wise, saffron-robed sage, with a beatific expression, sitting in a perfect yogic lotus posture, who seems entirely removed from worldly aspirations. Often, this picture comes with the false belief that enlightened beings are always and eternally established in bliss, in peace — and that no emotion could even create a ripple in their sublime stillness.

Others might have no clue, or hold no preconceptions, of what a so-called enlightened master *looks* like, but have beliefs about what enlightenment *is*. Some believe it means the end of all suffering, all judgments, including the end of anything that is not what we consider enlightened thinking or enlightened behavior.

Others believe enlightenment means you must be totally free, not bound by any of the rules of society, established in a benevolent love that allows you to act freely and lovingly toward all beings, and that no negative thought or belief could possibly penetrate this presence of grace.

Yet others believe that in order to be enlightened, you must annihilate the ego, penetrate the lie of worldly illusion, and that in one single, cataclysmic event you suddenly are enlightened — and remain that way for the rest of your life. It is as if some huge magical, liberative blasting has to take place, and then you suddenly *land* in final enlightenment.

Some spiritual teachers label this experience "smashing the pot" or receiving the "final cut."

Still others believe enlightenment is reserved only for the rare masters who have spent their entire lives in spiritual austerity — purifying their minds and bodies through rituals, mantras, yogas, and scriptures. Attaining enlightenment is so hard it is almost completely unavailable and unattainable by the normal, everyday householder.

Many see enlightenment as total detachment, where one is almost inhumanly disengaged from life. Once enlightened, a person does not respond in any way to the everyday sufferings that beset the rest of humanity, appearing emotionless, impassive, almost lifeless. This version usually includes the notion of "transcending" worldly life.

Some believe enlightenment requires you to live in poverty and complete austerity, serving humanity by helping others to awaken to their own purity.

Some even believe that with enlightenment come superhuman powers: mind reading, seeing into the future, astral projection, and other *siddhis*. With enlightenment, all desires are magically fulfilled, and disease cannot visit the body of the holy one.

And so it goes, on and on and on. Our mental constructs pile up as we try to imagine and project what it must be like to live in this ultimate state of bliss, paradise, nirvana. Often, our ideas coagulate around and magnify this notion called enlightenment until the whole thing seems so impossible, so distant — something that could only be attained in some far-off future, after having spent a lifetime doing everything we could to *earn* it or *attain* it.

Do you recognize what I am talking about? What ideas have *you* brought with you regarding enlightenment?

Why not let them come into your awareness right now. In fact, take a few moments to welcome every concept you've ever had about the subject of enlightenment, and if you like, you can write them down on a piece of paper. Write down what you think enlightenment is, what it looks like, how it behaves, and what you think you need to do to attain it, if it's even attainable.

When you're finished, and everything you believe is true about enlightenment has been brought into consciousness, ask yourself, "What if it was *all a lie? Just a huge* lie!"

What if *all* notions, ideas, and concepts about enlightenment are, in fact, *just that* . . . just *ideas* born from a mental construct of a projected ideal that you aspire to? What if everything you imagine to be true about enlightenment turned out to be just a fantasy born from a deep wish to experience the divine, the sublime, the infinite? What if every notion you ever held regarding enlightenment was just a dream? And what if the very act of creating these imaginary constructs and mental images was *preventing* you from experiencing the unobscured enlightenment that is *already* here — the vast, boundless, infinite presence that is your own essence?

What if there was *nothing* to attain? What if you are already resting in an ocean of enlightened awareness, but you can't see it because you're too busy looking for something "out there" — that ideal, that paradise, that nirvana? What if infinite presence is already waiting *inside*, calling you *home* to yourself?

What if there was nothing you could do to attain enlightenment? And what if enlightenment is only revealed in the not doing, in effortless being?

Let's try an experiment right now. Imagine taking *all* of your notions, images, and mental constructs and putting a huge red *X* right through them. If you've written them down on paper, do exactly that — cross them out with a big *X*. Then imagine bundling all those beautifully crafted concepts into a nice sack and burning them. If you've written them on paper, you can literally burn them or rip them up and toss them in the trash.

Once all constructs have disappeared, all mind talk is gone, all idyllic notions have dissolved — when all ideas have vanished — what remains?

Really *experience* this — even for just a moment. At the end of this paragraph, stop reading and take a moment to be still. Experience what it is like when consciousness is free from all mental activity. Take a few deep breaths and experience thought-free awareness . . .

What remains? What is left when all thought has come and all thought has gone? What truly remains? Is this vast, spacious awareness touched in any way by the ideas that have come and gone through it? Or does it remain totally free, whole, complete?

Check for yourself . . . When all thoughts have been welcomed, and naturally fade away, what remains?

If you are really innocent and open — if you take a moment to pause, breathe, and be still — you will experience unobscured freedom, nothingness, vastness . . . pure presence, enlightened awareness.

Enlightened awareness is experienced as being here when all thoughts, constructs, and ideas have been removed, let go of. It is revealed to be the wide, open field *in which* all thoughts appear and disappear.

You didn't have to do any mantras or practices, or perform any great austerities or *sadhana* to get this — for this open presence is your own nature. It's already whole; it's already completely attained! As a matter of fact, any efforting to *try* to attain it only pushes the direct experience of it further into the distance.

It's only when you *stop*, breathe, open, and welcome all thought — really welcome it — that thought is free to come to rest. It's free to come and it's free to go, and *you* can rest in the vast, open presence through which it is appearing.

Something is welcoming thought: some huge, empty presence is the welcomer. That presence is your own self, your own essence — and any mental constructs, beliefs, mind talk, or images that come through it are simply that, thoughts, a bunch of words and images traveling through consciousness.

You are the consciousness through which all is coming and all is going. So, whether those ideas are right or wrong doesn't matter — they are just syllables trailing through awareness, through the boundless freedom that you already are.

Enlightenment is always here, always available. It is who *you are*.

✦

I REMEMBER HEARING A DELIGHTFUL STORY that drove home to me how fruitless it is to go searching for enlightenment.

It is an old story, one passed from teacher to student, and over the years I have heard many variations of it, but it is always a fresh reminder to call off the search and experience what is here right now.

So, once again, you might like to get comfortable, relax, and feel yourself opening as you read a story that will remind you of the ocean of grace that you are already resting in.

✦

ONCE UPON A TIME, there was a very young, playful wave. This wave had lots of character and was full of fun; it loved to bubble and effervesce and dance in various circular motions. It delighted totally in its wavelike existence.

One day, the young wave was making some particularly mischievous movements when he heard a deep, almost imperceptible sound coming from the very depths: "Ocean," it said.

Upon hearing this deep, resonant sound, something stirred in the wave's being, and he felt a strong pull from the most primal part of himself to understand its meaning. It sounded compellingly mysterious, and the young wave just couldn't stop thinking about it.

His thirst to understand this mystery grew and grew, and when a dolphin passed nearby, the young wave asked for some advice, "Oh, dolphin, before you go — you've always seemed so smart, so clever — can you tell me something? I heard that there is something called 'ocean,' only I don't know what it means, or where it is. Can you tell me?"

The dolphin squeaked back that he'd been hearing everyone talk about it for some time, and that there were a few

theories floating around about what it must be like — there
were even some older, scholarly dolphins who held regular
meetings to try to understand its meaning — but no one had
yet discovered the truth of it: the concept was still at the ideas
stage.

The dolphin wished the young wave blessings and flipped
his flipper good-bye as he laughed and shouted, "Good luck.
Maybe you'll be the first one to discover the great mystery."
And then he frolicked out of sight.

Later that day an old sea turtle came drifting by, and the
young wave perked up and asked the ancient one the same
question. Figuring that this turtle had probably grown wise
in his long years, the wave hoped he might know the answer
to his mystery.

"Oh turtle, surely you've traveled and seen much over
your many years. And I am but a young wave and have not
the benefit of your experience. So, please, can you tell me,
have you ever heard of the ocean? Have you ever seen it?
Every time I hear the word arising inside, it stirs something
deep within. I *must* come to understand it, to experience it.
Please can you help me, old wise one?"

The turtle listened quietly to the impetuous wave, and
answered in a slow, low voice, "Oh son, that is a question I
myself have been pondering for, lo, these many years. But,
honestly, I can't say I've ever seen it. I can't even say I know
what it is. I sense there is a deep secret, and many have developed complex theories about its nature, but I can't say that I've
actually got any real knowledge of it. No, son, like me, I fear
you may spend the rest of your days searching for the answer.

"I wish you good fortune, young one. You have your whole life ahead of you; perhaps you'll be the rare and lucky one to find the true experience of the ocean."

The young wave felt saddened that he was having so little success with his quest to find the ocean, and he feared that maybe no one could really give him an answer.

The next day a big, old, well-formed wave came rolling in his direction. Excited, thinking that surely this majestic grandfather wave *must* have the answer, the little wave asked spiritedly, "Oh, great wave — you are old and wise and have lived much longer than I. I've heard a rumbling from somewhere deep inside, and the word 'ocean' keeps haunting me. I *have* to find it. I simply *must* find the answer to my mystery. What is it? Where can I find it?"

The old wave sighed a deep sigh: "Oh, young one, this is a question that only the wisest of the wise ask. You must be a very special wave that you have such a deep spiritual calling to understand the mysteries of the ocean. I wish I could help you, but I have been traveling all of my days, and while my thirst to find the ocean has never left me, try as I might, I've never fathomed its meaning.

"Oh, many have *thought* they had figured it out, and others have constructed complicated theories. Everyone agrees that the truth of it must be nearly impossible to attain, and I've certainly never experienced it. In all honesty, I'm not even sure it really exists."

The little wave sank in disappointment. Sensing the young wave's sadness, the big wave made a bold invitation. "Listen, young one, why don't you travel with me? If we go on this quest together, perhaps the mystery will finally unfold; maybe the secret will be revealed. I keep feeling in the very depths of my being that the presence of the ocean is very close — if only I could grasp it. Let's travel together, and we'll see what life brings us."

And so they did: the young, perky, playful wave building its strength and volume as it traveled alongside the great, old, wise wave.

After many miles they both began to feel a current from deep within; they sensed their journey quickening. In complete surrender they let themselves open into the power that was mysteriously building from the depths.

Then they spied in the distance something never before experienced, but something they'd heard whispered about between the fishes. The old wave said, "My goodness! That must be what the fishes call 'the shore' and 'the land beyond.' I never thought I'd actually see it in my lifetime!"

The power inside became even stronger, and as they came closer and closer to the shore, a compelling surge drove them both faster, and faster, and faster toward the beach. They picked up more and more speed until, suddenly, *crash!* All bubbling, foaming, splashing, they openly surrendered, and they both merged back into the ocean from where they'd come. In that instant they realized: they'd always *been* the ocean — it was their very essence. They were made from it. They were infused with the infinite presence of it. It had always been their true nature. It was just that, in the past, they'd only identified with being the wave *on top* of the ocean. Now they knew they'd always been and always would be the vast, boundless ocean itself. It was their essence.

✦

YOU ARE THIS OCEAN. It is your essence. You *are* the very enlightenment you have been seeking.

It's time to call off the search, and just rest in the infinite presence that has always been and will always be *who you already are.*

Let the whole play of mind come to dance on your surface. Even though thoughts, like waves, arise from the ocean of being, they are *not* the ocean itself. Instead, like waves, they are free to come and free to go: the depths of the ocean remain completely undisturbed by all the drama of life parading through it. You are the ocean — the infinite ocean of enlightenment.

✦

LIKE THE LITTLE WAVE, and like many spiritual seekers, I too spent most of my younger years thirsting, seeking, longing to experience enlightenment and to merge into the divine. I went from teachers to masters, to yogis, to monasteries, to ashrams. I traversed many spiritual traditions, read all the right texts, performed endless austerities, fasts, practices, and mantras — but nothing could seem to slake my thirst or provide an ongoing, everlasting, direct realization of infinite presence.

Along the way, I learned countless theories and developed my own beliefs about enlightenment. I thought it could only be attained through endless practice, fervent desire, total surrender, and complete focus on the goal 100 percent of the time. I sat with several enlightened masters, and in their wakeful presence I experienced many awakenings in which I bathed in the bliss of freedom. But even while basking in scintillating presence, steeping in love, the longing still burned and I kept searching. Sometimes I thought I might die in the ferocity of its blaze. In fact, I was willing to physically die if it meant merging into God and realizing self.

Even though grace was surrounding me, embracing me, shining in everything, I *still* held onto the notion that enlightenment had to be *attained*, that it was somewhere "out there," and my realization of it would happen at some time in the future.

I pigeonholed these sublime experiences, categorized them as mere passing states, letting them become mere beautiful, faded memories. I renounced these experiences as not *true* enlightenment and kept my focus and attention on my imagined goal, one that matched my ideal picture of what I *believed* enlightenment must be like, overlooking the finite presence I was already steeping in! With my arrogant certitudes about enlightenment, I had put myself on a path of postponement. An egotistical expertise had arisen, and I had fallen into the absolute belief that I had become acutely discerning: I *knew* what enlightenment was supposed to *look* like, *sound* like, and *feel* like, and this knowing caused me to miss it when it was standing right before my eyes.

Like the little wave, I was already soaking in it, but I was still reaching outside, trying to find it, to experience it, to fathom its mystery. Then one day, like the wave, I had a wonderful collision with reality, and a cataclysmic realization that finally crashed through my world of the known. In that one moment, all my ideas fell away: my beliefs about who I thought I was, my identification with a constructed somebody I'd come to believe was my self — for one instant all my preconceived notions of enlightenment completely dropped away. And in that moment I saw through the lie of my search.

Through the course of my spiritual seeking, I have been blessed to sit with many extraordinary teachers, and I ended up spending seven years at the feet of a particularly sublime and radiant enlightened master — Gurumayi. In her presence, everything became alive with a scintillating grace. The very atmosphere seemed saturated with it. In her presence, even the most ordinary and simple of rooms would appear glorious, resplendent, and permeated with peace.

I surrendered myself totally to that grace, and like many of her students, I learned how to serve truth in each moment as I offered all of myself in selfless service in her ashrams and centers. Through the course of those years I had countless awakenings, revelations, realizations, experiences of bliss — and I had no doubt that I was sitting with a true master, in the presence of enlightenment.

I felt myself to be the luckiest person alive, and holding onto my concrete belief that enlightenment was available "out there, sometime in the future," the ferocity of my devotion to freedom only became fiercer and fiercer. The longing to merge into God, into grace, became almost unbearable. This longing was taking place even while I was resting in bliss. It would not cease. When I went to bed, it was burning; when I awoke, it was the first experience of the day.

My husband, who shared this great love of truth, had a thirst to experience self-inquiry (*advaita*), and longed to learn from a true *jnani* master. He had heard of an old enlightened teacher who had been "fully realized" for over fifty years, and who lived in a very humble village north of Delhi in India.

The master was considered by many to be the final teacher. In his presence, many students were reported to have become liberated, and several enlightened teachers still came to sit with him, for his intellect was piercing, and he could penetrate any concepts or ideas of separation that might be surreptitiously hanging about in consciousness. Poonjaji, also affectionately known as Papaji, though living an extremely modest life, was reputed to be the final step in one's journey to enlightenment.

But I felt completely graced in Gurumayi's presence and did not share my husband's desire to meet Papaji. It was only out of marital devotion that I accompanied him to Lucknow, to sit with this venerated teacher.

Whether Papaji deserved his reputation, I didn't know. Ultimately, I secretly believed that no one could *really* attain enlightenment — you had to have it *bestowed* upon you, as a final descent of grace from the teacher whom you'd spent years serving, and in whose presence, through practices and austerities, your being and body had become totally purified. I'd already chosen my path: my *sadhana* was firmly established in Gurumayi's teachings, and I was interested in no other master. She was my beloved teacher, and I trusted her utterly and lived her teachings as my life.

So, with little interest and mild skepticism, I arrived with my husband in the dusty northern Indian village where the great master Poonjaji lived. The place was full of poverty, sickness, mangy dogs, pigs living in open sewers, overworked and exhausted horses, and pollution-choked air. I wondered, "What the heck am I doing here?" Papaji's village had nothing sublime about it. Though I'd grown to love India over the years, to my Western eyes, this village looked like a cesspool.

I was used to sitting with Gurumayi in her Ganeshpuri Ashram in south India, which was an exquisite monastery, set in paradisiacal botanical gardens. It was picturesque, pristine, resplendent with devotion — nothing like this filthy, grimy, stinking, impossibly hot village with no air to breathe.

The morning after we arrived, we stood in a long queue to get into Papaji's satsang hall. Everyone was huddled around the front door, impatient to get into the small hall, which could hold only about two hundred students. It seemed to my eyes that no one had even bothered to dress for the occasion. I was accustomed to waiting for the master in long, orderly queues, where everyone was respectful and quiet with anticipation, where everyone was freshly bathed and dressed in their Sunday best to honor the occasion and to show our respect. At best, this was a motley, disheveled, and disorganized group.

I wasn't impressed. I had a long list of rules about how to behave around a master, and these people appeared not to know the simplest teachings about honoring themselves, each other, or the teacher.

When the front door opened, everyone flooded through like a teeming brawl. Pushing to find seats, everyone scrambled to get close to the front, and the satsang hall was completely packed with people sitting on a stone floor, knee to knee — practically in each other's laps. At one point we were asked to move as far forward as possible, to make room for others still standing outside the door, and so we all crammed together like so many sardines. Everyone's body was touching someone else's. My sense of personal space was uncomfortably encroached upon — there was way too much body contact for my more austere sensibilities. Nothing matched my vision of spiritual decorum.

My mind was flooded with nothing but judgments. "Is this the way to behave in the presence of a venerated master?" I thought. I was so arrogant, so superior. I *knew for certain* the respectful protocol for sitting with a teacher, and to my eyes these bedraggled, hippie wanderers from around the world didn't have a clue how to behave.

Papaji entered the hall very quietly and unassumingly, without any fanfare, and a ripple went through the audience. Everyone settled and became still.

Papaji's demeanor was humble, open, not studied or practiced in any way. He seemed totally at ease, and he laughed often and deeply. Most of what he said I had heard before, and I was somewhat shocked at some of the seemingly irreverent questions asked by some of the students. Didn't they know who they were sitting with? Sitting with an enlightened master is the rarest, most priceless of experiences. These students seemed more fond of hearing their own voices than that of the master. The whole session seemed a shambles compared with the restrained, quiet, planned, orderly, pristine, and formal satsangs I was accustomed to.

Because I was so full of all my preconceptions about how to behave, I couldn't see the deep devotion burning in many people's eyes. I couldn't feel the still presence emanating from them, nor could I sense the power of their commitment to truth.

At the end of the session, we all stood. I was soaking in a blaze of burning stillness, and we put our hands in prayer position to honor Papaji as he left the hall. As he was passing by he looked me deeply in the eyes, and then he turned to my husband and spontaneously invited us to lunch at his home.

Shocked, nonplussed, I looked at the other students around me. Wasn't he going to invite them? It appeared not. I felt a little embarrassed and yet simultaneously blessed beyond words. We followed him to his car, waved good-bye, and then walked down the dusty road to his house.

When we arrived, we entered a combined living room/dining room area that was simpler than any I'd ever seen — just a plain Formica-topped table with a plastic tablecloth and old chairs from the fifties. Ordinary, somewhat worn, and unmatched floor cushions lined the walls of a tiny lounge. A flickering fluorescent lamp lit this spartan room, whose only distinguishing decorative features were some pictures of places and saints that Papaji had gathered on his many travels.

Papaji was eighty-two years old, and he hobbled to his dining table and quietly read through a stack of letters from ardent seekers asking spiritual questions. He motioned for my husband and me to sit down at the end of the table, asked a few polite-seeming questions about how we'd come to meet him, and then turned his attention back to his mail. Finally, lunch arrived, and we ate a simple, lovingly prepared meal, without any prayers or special offerings.

Papaji certainly did not fit the popular stereotype of a spiritual master. He'd changed out of his traditional *kurta* (a simple long shirt with a Nehru collar and matching white trousers), and he was now wearing a clean though somewhat tattered T-shirt bearing the words "Byron Bay." I figured someone must have given it to him long before, perhaps to entice him to visit Australia. There was nothing glamorous, monklike, or ascetic about him. He looked perfectly *ordinary*, even plain — like anybody's grandfather sitting at his kitchen table.

Above us on the wall was an old-fashioned television set — one that, we learned, frequently went on the blink, as did the electricity in the house from time to time. No sacred halls, no quietly robed monks serving him, no pomp or circumstance — just an old man sitting in a modest room in an impoverished Indian village.

Yet this was the "teachers' teacher," the gurus' guru. It didn't make any sense to my *eyes*.

Papaji invited us to stay at his house for our entire visit. As he was currently on a special fast in honor of a holy celebration, we joined him. We ate only raw fruit and vegetables (washed in disinfectant, as this was India). This was fine for me, as I had undergone many fasts in my life.

Why we were invited, I didn't know. What we were supposed to learn wasn't apparent. Although he gave daily satsang at the meeting hall, Papaji wasn't giving any formal teachings at the house, so while there, we pretty much sat watching an octogenarian go about living a quiet, mundane-seeming life.

At times Papaji seemed to get grumpy. In the next moment, he might laugh to himself about something ironic he'd just read in a letter. Irritation came and went. Impatience arose and subsided. If a letter arrived that was deeply moving, he would sit and cry at the beauty of it. The whole panoply of human emotion seemed to play through his consciousness. Yet, like an infant who feels emotion freely and easily, none of it seemed to stick. It was as if the emotion arose, was felt, and passed cleanly through, and the stillness remained untouched by it.

Day after day we sat quietly. Sometimes we spoke, sometimes people came to deliver things and were invited in, but as we were on a fast, Papaji didn't invite others in for meals. There were just a handful of people preparing raw food, cleaning, tending to the needs of the house, while Papaji sat in silence or watched cricket and wrestling on Indian television. Sometimes, a movie on the Ramayana or Mahabharata would come on as a special program in the evening, but there was nothing remarkable-seeming about any of it. Everything was so human, so real, so normal.

On the fifth day of our fast, as we were sitting in silence, a thought suddenly arose: "What am I doing here in this house watching an old man who has a penchant for loud Indian television?" Then the next thought arose, "Oh, my God — that's the first thought I've had in five days!"

I had been resting so quietly in thought-free awareness that it hadn't even occurred to me to question it — it was so natural, so unremarkable, so ordinary, as if resting in pure presence had always been the only experience I had ever known. There was no running commentary going on internally, no mental grasping, grappling, resisting, or ideation. I was saturated in pure peace, and I hadn't even noticed it because my thinking mind had come to rest and there was no one there to comment on it; just pure awareness being itself.

There hadn't been some huge thunderbolt or any crashing experience of awakening. I was just resting in thought-free stillness, and it was as natural as brushing my teeth.

All of my ideas of what enlightenment was supposed to "look" like and how I should behave and act had melted away into nothingness, and I was left as pristine awareness.

At the end of the fast, I finally put pen to paper and wrote a letter to Papaji, begging for final enlightenment — I wanted to merge into God. It seemed partly absurd, because who would merge into what I didn't know — for everything was alive as consciousness. But, somehow, I still thought that I needed a final blasting realization and bestowal of grace in order to attain enlightenment, so that is what I asked for.

What took place over the next several days was not just the experience of a one-off blasting realization, but more a simple stripping away of all the lies, illusions, identifications, fantasies, judgments, rules, beliefs, and concepts that I had about enlightenment. Patiently, Papaji peeled away all the concepts, until all that remained was pure awareness. Sometimes, he turned my acquired knowledge upside down and inside out, until we both just laughed at the absurdity of it. At other times, he asked me to inquire into the reality, into the truth, of the nature of my ideas and beliefs, and they were seen to be nothing but empty, insubstantial concepts.

At other times, when I was speaking about previous revelations and powerful kundalini experiences, he would ask, "Are these experiences here right now?"

"No, Papaji," I would answer. And he would reply, "This that comes and this that goes is *not real*. You abide in this that *always* remains — in reality: in the eternal presence that does not come and does not go."

Like so many sandcastles, the concepts dissolved, until the whole notion that there ever was a separate somebody called Brandon came into question. That, too, was realized to be just another idea — and when the lie of that illusion was penetrated, all the legs holding up the table called "enlightenment" finally collapsed, and the game of believing in an enlightenment "out there" was finished.

Papaji didn't give me some huge, final teaching. He penetrated all the lies and limitations I'd created regarding enlightenment. It was not a time of addition, but one of subtraction. Instead of *giving* me teachings, practices, mantras, and beliefs, *he took them all away.* What remained was unobscured awareness, pure presence, radiant emptiness.

He told me that the only difference between one who is enlightened and one who is not is belief: the certain belief that you are *not* enlightened is what keeps you from experiencing the infinite presence that is always here. When you simply realize that enlightenment is always here, then everywhere you look, there it is: you can't avoid it.

When all identifications, beliefs, concepts, and theories were gone, everything that had been obscuring open awareness became *obviously apparent.* I'd overlooked the obvious because my focus had always been elsewhere! All along, this that I had been seeking was already *here.*

I realized that I was resting in an ocean of grace, pure presence, unobscured freedom, and I'd spent my whole life in this embrace. It wasn't somewhere "out there," in my future. It was *right* here, surrounding, suffusing, and shining in everything. I'd simply overlooked it! I realized it was here the instant I got fully present to it. Once I stopped labeling it as a past experience, stopped imagining what it might be like in the future, stopped all the mind games, and just innocently opened into the present moment — unobscured awareness was realized to be here. In fact, I experienced it as being everywhere, in everything.

What a joke! All my life I'd spent in fruitless searching, when what I was seeking was closer than my own breath. And I didn't even have to *do* anything to get it. In fact, it was my very "doing" that had taken me *away* from it!

From that day forward I ceased seeking and decided it

was time to just relax, to rest in the open presence that is shining here, available each and every moment, whenever you bring your awareness to it.

I hadn't recognized it, but somehow I'd fostered a notion that enlightenment was a landing place — that you landed there and suddenly and forever you resided there, in enlightenment, realization.

I didn't know then what I do now: that enlightenment is simply an invitation to open and be fully present in this moment — with no thought of past, and no thought of future — just this moment. It's fully and completely available each time you bring your awareness to the now. It can't go anywhere because it is your self. You can let your attention wander and let your mind collapse into some other notion or concept, but the moment you stop, open, and just be still, everything you are seeking is realized to be already here.

I came to realize that enlightenment is a continual opening: concepts can't cling to it, lies burn away in it, dramas get played out through it, and the whole dance of life is happening in it — waking, sleeping, all of life takes place in this vast embrace. Sometimes, when my awareness collapses into some story, I still get lost in the drama of something "out there," and I believe myself to be the wave. I get caught up in the wave's unique movements and ever-changing patterns for a brief time, and in those moments, the ocean fades into the background, and the drama on the surface takes center stage. But the second I stop, drop the story and my belief in it, the ocean pulls me back into itself — into an endless sea of peace. I realize its presence was there all along, even when I pretended for a moment to get involved in the game and played at being a little wave.

Of course, its presence is always here. How can the ocean go anywhere? It's what you are made of, who you are. Wherever you go, there it is — and all thoughts, dramas, the full dance of life, are merely waves on the surface of this that is your infinite self.

Since the day I penetrated the lie of my illusory search and realized that I am this ocean, it has become increasingly difficult to buy into the drama dancing on the surface for any time. For me, the reality of this moment and the power of its presence is too strong a pull to resist — it keeps calling me back into itself.

These days I find the drama of life may still dance through — it just seems to be happening in a vaster presence of grace. Thoughts come and go in it, feelings are welcome in it — in fact, all of life is welcome in it — yet the infinite presence does not come and *does not* go.

What if *you* were to finally drop all of your notions, let go of all your ideas, and relinquish all your judgments? What if *you* decided to discover what remains when all your ideas of what enlightenment is, and is not, are stripped away?

What would you discover?

Enlightened awareness is the pristine presence that remains after all ideas have fallen away. It is your very essence, who you are and who you will always be.

You have always been enlightened. Give up the belief that you are not, and rest as what is. Do not question it. Do not quantify it. Don't touch it. Just be still in it.

Truth is. Peace is. Life is.
It is time to call off the search.
You are this that you have been seeking.

✦

YESTERDAY, I RAN INTO A RADIANT YOUNG MAN who appeared to be in his midtwenties. He seemed to have a clear, sharp mind, and it was obvious that he was a fervent spiritual seeker.

He stopped me just as I was leaving a friend's house to continue writing this book. I was already running late and didn't want to stop to have a conversation, but something in the young man's eyes made me stop, just as I had my foot out of the front door.

"Do you mind if I ask you a spiritual question?" he asked.

I hesitated, taking a moment to meet his intense eyes. There was a burning urgency there — a genuine longing to find an answer to a real spiritual question — and compassion flooded my being. He looked like I imagine I must have appeared so often to my teachers — thirsty, hungry, searching for true answers to deep questions.

I paused, my heart melted, and I replied, "Well, we'll see what arises." Then I added gently, "Is it possible we can make it brief? I'm actually in a bit of a rush."

The young man struggled internally to find a way to make his question clear and succinct, to get right to the core of the issue. He stammered a bit, then a rush of words came tumbling out, punctuated with pauses, stops, and starts: "In enlightenment...I mean, when someone is enlightened... they don't have any preferences, do they? I mean...they view everything as the same, don't they? If they're *really* enlightened, they don't judge if something is different from something else...do they?"

I stood still, looking into his eyes, and was getting ready to reply, when more words came tumbling out: "I mean, like when I go to the shopping mall...I prefer some things and I don't like others...and some things I see there are so commercial that I dislike them...and sometimes I see people doing things there that I don't think are right... And, well ...judgment comes in. But, in enlightenment... does judgment ever arise in enlightenment...if you're *really* enlightened?"

He stumbled a bit more, trying to further articulate his question, until finally I asked, "So, when you go to the mall, you find you have preferences and that judgment arises? Is that it?"

"Well, yes...but does it happen in enlightenment?"

Briefly, I remembered some of the various enlightened masters I'd sat with, and internally I smiled. They didn't just have preferences, they had *strong* preferences, and they often expressed them loud and clear to all who would listen.

I asked, "By enlightenment, you mean this vast, empty field of presence that is here?" I indicated a spaciousness with my hands, as if it were already surrounding us, embracing us.

"Well...yes. But do differences show up in it?"

"All kinds of preferences show up in it — judgments come and go. Strong emotions come and go. Likes and dislikes come and go. But this infinite presence is not touched by anything. It sounds like you are *judging* your judgments... Are you?"

He nodded his head, and I saw something slotting into place. "So, what if you stopped judging what came through this enlightenment? What if, instead, you welcomed all your judgments *into* it? Has it occurred to you that perhaps these judgments are longing for freedom, and that they are coming up for satsang, to taste enlightenment? Our judgments long for freedom, just like everything else does.

"What if you were to do something radical, right now? Just stop for a moment, become aware of the spaciousness already here, and ask for all the judgments to come flooding. Really welcome them..."

For a moment he stared into space, as his awareness turned inward. Then his body visibly relaxed as he genuinely welcomed his judgments. While he was welcoming them, I said, "You know what? Just welcome *all* judgments into this love, this freedom — not just particular ones, but *all* of them, all of mankind's judgments, even your ancestors' judgments. Stay spacious, stay open. Now, is enlightenment — is this spacious love touched by any of your judgments?"

"No... I get it... No, it's not."

"Who is it that is welcoming the judgments?"

He visibly opened his being, and answered, "I am."

"Yes, you are the welcomer — you are the infinite field that is welcoming all judgment into spaciousness.

"So, when no resistance is here; when all welcome is here — is there any problem with judgments?" I asked.

"No..." he said, quite incredulously. "No...no problem at all."

"Perhaps your judgments just needed a little love. Perhaps all they needed was to be welcomed into the love. Are they any problem to this field of love?"

"No...not at all."

"So, why don't you just *love* all your judgments? Just welcome them all into this love while you remain *as* this field of love — untouched by anything that comes through it. All kinds of things come through this enlightenment, you know — emotions, thoughts, judgments, preferences — but can you experience that this that you are is untouched by anything coming through?"

He opened further.

"Yes...yes, I can."

"Well, I have an assignment for you. After I leave, go take a few minutes to sit quietly in this vast openness, and just welcome every judgment you've ever had into this love. Discover for yourself what *remains* untouched. Just love your judgments to death...Love them to death."

He smiled at the metaphor, recognized its true meaning, nodded approval, and agreed that he would do exactly that.

And I have no doubt that he did. And I'm sure he loved them to death.

This love is such a vast, open field — it makes no judgments about what comes through it, and as a result no resistance arises. It's only when you think something *shouldn't* be there, and try to push it away or judge it, that resistance arises.

He *was* right. In enlightened awareness, love makes no distinction. It accepts all, and allows everything to come through — and it's unstained, untainted, and untouched by any of it.

It just depends — do you identify with the thoughts and judgments, or do you open and let them pass through the vaster context of your being? The choice is yours: enlightenment is always present, always available, no matter what choices you make. It loves you that much.

✦

OVER THE YEARS since that first stripping away, I came to realize that the subtracting, the letting go, the falling away, the "dying," is an ongoing, never-ending process. As identifications, resistances, tendencies, and mind games continue to be consumed by grace, the realization of this boundless presence deepens. Purification is *still* happening — it's just happening in the vaster context of grace: the grace of freedom.

Enlightenment is not a one-off experience, or a landing place, but an endless opening into the infinite.

In this ocean of love, I still enjoy singing, chanting, dancing, prayer, yoga, and meditation — *not* because they will cause me to attain something called "enlightenment," but just because bliss arises and my being enjoys it. I have no illusions that these activities will give me anything, but it is joyful to experience them nonetheless. I love singing and chanting — it opens up the heart. I adore sitting quietly in nature, and meditation happens naturally, of its own accord.

It's not something I do formally as a practice; it just arises as a pull from within, and the eyes close, and I just rest.

The realizations continue to come: experiences of kundalini are endless. Awakenings and openings continue to happen. They all just arise in the vaster context of being.

And something deepens. Papaji gave me clear instructions that as I was resting in open awareness, unborn potential, I was not to take up residence as anything — especially not enlightenment, for that too is a trap.

Just be content to rest in this unknown, free from all labels, constructs, and ideas.

Over the years, many people have asked me, "Are you enlightened, Brandon?" I can only answer, "I don't know." In order to think about it, I would have to take up residence in some concept of enlightenment — as a some*body* who attained some*thing*. It all seems too effortful, and would only cause separation. I prefer not to rest as anything but pure awareness. I'm content to be in the unknown. Enlightenment already is: I don't need to take up residence as it. It's already shining everywhere.

You too can relax in this vast unknown and give up your ideas of enlightenment. It's not a landing place — just an endless opening into this infinite embrace.

Guided Introspection: Self-Inquiry

For this contemplation, you can use the companion CD (see page 221) or simply read it through and do it on your own.

This simple process of self-inquiry is designed to penetrate the lies of who we think we are, and to open us into the truth of who we really are. It is a simple question, but it is the most powerful and profound one I know, for it can give you a direct experience of your infinite self, causing you to penetrate the labels you've come to identify yourself with.

In the beginning, in response to the question, your roles and labels may arise. But if you stay open and continue to inquire, eventually all your old identities will fall away and what will remain is unobscured awareness, freedom, your self. The experience of the self most often arises as a wordless response. It comes as a direct experience of vast spaciousness, of open stillness, of boundlessness.

For this contemplation, all you need to do is continue asking the question and allow it to pull you deeper into yourself.

You are already free and completely whole. Your essence is vast and spacious, and the enlightened awareness you've been seeking is already present. It is calling you home to your self… right now.

There is nothing you can do to attain it, so just relax… for it is already here… it is who you are. Enlightened awareness is your own essence, and when all labels fall away, this pristine presence is all that remains.

So, find a quiet comfortable space where you can sit uninterrupted.

You might like to take a few deep breaths in… and slowly exhale… Deep breath in… and slowly let it out… Slow breath in… and let it out.

Then when you're ready, you may close your eyes, letting yourself become still and spacious… Let your awareness open spaciously in front… become vast behind… and infinite to all sides… boundless below… and spacious above.

And just rest as an ocean of awareness.

Innocently begin asking yourself, "Who am I?"

Allowing whatever response arises to come up naturally…
open and again ask, "Who am I?" Remain open to directly experience the response rising from within.

Continue asking, "Who am I?…Who am I *really?*" — until all
labels fall away…Then discover what remains — this ocean of
awareness. Continue repeating the question…and it will carry
you deeper into the boundlessness.

Continue asking until all is vast and spacious…and just
rest…just soak…steep in your own presence…in the infinite
ocean of your self.

And when you are ready, you may open your eyes.

✦

Freedom already *is.*
It's who you are, who you always will be.
It's time to live in the freedom that is already here.
It's time to live a life of grace.

ACKNOWLEDGMENTS

So many extraordinary people have contributed to Journeywork around the world, and I couldn't possibly name them all here. But with all my heart I thank the thousands of beautiful souls whose fierce love of truth and healing brought them to Journey seminars, to dive in and fully experience the in-depth work. To those who are now offering these tools for transformation and freedom to humanity: you are the real awakeners, the torchbearers, and we all owe you a debt of gratitude.

I also thank our core Journey team from our offices around the world. You are models of grace in action. Your surrender to truth and selfless service to humanity take my breath away. I bow to you with all my heart. One of the greatest blessings of my life is that I am surrounded by rare quality beings. Everyone who comes to Journey seminars is graced by your devotion, love, and integrity. I will never stop saying thank you for your generous hearts.

In the United States and Canada, huge love and gratitude to Skip, Kristine, Michelle, and their staff, as well as the Journey ambassadors who work so cohesively and beautifully in getting the word out. Thank you all for your passion, dedication, and all your love.

From the bottom of my heart I thank those in the European offices: Gaby, Cliff, Claire, Arnold, Tricia, Julia, Richard, Joanne, Sarah, Kaye, Debs, Joel, Anna-Eva, Bettina, Jane, Melanie-Grace, and the many others who help out there.

Great love and gratitude to the Australasian team: Laurie, Katrina, Anné, Mollie, Charlene, Nada, Bill, Phill, Sharon, Satya, Janet, Janine, Yollana, Roy, Yantra, Vanessa, Berislava, and the many others who support the team.

In South Africa, deep gratitude to Faizel, Lisa, Li, and their staff, as well as Rolene, Lydia, John, and the extended Journey family that makes it all possible.

Huge gratitude to all those who have contributed to Journey Outreach, and particularly those, including the outreach ambassadors, who actively volunteer in underprivileged communities around the world, bringing transformation and healing to all they touch. Special thanks to the Journey Outreach board members, who serve selflessly and unconditionally, asking for nothing more than a smile in return. Carolyn, Bill, Phill, Debbie, Paul, Faizel, Gaby, Kevin, and Jan: you are bright beacons and models to us all.

And the worldwide embrace would not be complete without mentioning the amazing Journey Accredited Practitioners, who work with dedication, openness, and love. You are a grace-filled gift to the world. Thank you for your support in making available the deeper work, and thank you for continuing to offer yourself into the fire of liberation.

Thank you all!

I would especially like to thank Marc Allen, Georgia Hughes, Munro Magruder, and the whole team at New World Library. Your warm welcome, enthusiasm, and openness make us all feel grateful to be partnering with you. Your care, creativity, and tireless attention to detail in the editing and design of this book are deeply appreciated.

I would also like to thank Denis Campbell for your vision, passion, and dedication in getting this book into publishers' hands in so many countries. You have worked day and night with the prayer that this work gets into as many homes as possible. Your enthusiasm has opened many doors and many hearts.

And to Manfred and Sue, our agents at Inter License: I don't know how to thank you enough for your faith, care, dedication, and support. Thank you. Thank you. Thank you.

On the personal front, I offer my deepest thanks to Kevin Billett, my life partner, managing director of The Journey International, and the real editor of this work — in fact, the editor of all Journeywork.

This book would not have been possible without your meticulous eye, forever holding the content to the highest standard of truth and integrity. Your expertise at cutting away the inessential and exposing the shining, simple truth allows us all to experience that truth from within ourselves. You truly are an editor-in-grace. It is the greatest gift of my life to be allowed to stand alongside you and serve humanity in this love. Your fierce love of freedom blows me away, and each day spent in your company is a blessed day.

And most important, I must thank the teachers and masters who have pointed me deeper into freedom, cutting away lies, illusions, and concepts, opening me into this eternal presence. I bow to those teachers, known and not known, whose presence is guiding the huge wave of awakening that is sweeping the globe. There are those who have played immensely powerful roles in my life, and a few must be mentioned here. My deep gratitude to Gurumayi, a living experience of enlightenment, whose grace continues to live on in my very cells. Thank you with all my heart. Deep gratitude to you, Gangaji, for your fierce love and truth speaking, and to the fire of freedom alive in your presence. And to Papaji (Poonjaji), I don't know how to express my thanks. My heart overflows each moment in gratitude for your grace. I will never be able to thank you enough for being such a ruthless fire; for constantly stripping away, consuming all the ideas of who I thought I was; for leaving me no place to land; for forever opening and deepening me in this ocean of love. May every breath be lived as a never-ending prayer of gratitude to your grace. And endless love and gratitude to Ramana Maharshi, who lives in my heart as my heart, and is the whole reason for being. May your grace continue to liberate thousands of souls.

And finally, my gratitude to the unseen presence of grace pervading all of life; a grace so benevolent it brought me to the feet of these teachers and continues to consume everything that is not yet free.

I pray with all my heart that grace continues to burn through anything and everything that obscures, until there is nothing and no one left — just grace itself. May we all live in the embrace of freedom and grace.

ABOUT THE AUTHOR

Author of the international bestseller *The Journey* and *The Journey for Kids*, Brandon Bays is an American teacher who offers her hugely popular seminars and retreats in many countries around the world. Her teachings of spiritual awakening and healing have transformed the lives of hundreds of thousands. Brandon's style is direct and practical; she does not just point the way to the truth of the boundless, limitless self — instead, she gives step-by-step methods, practical tools that can be used easily and effectively on a daily basis.

Brandon's teachings evolved from her own spiritual realization and her experience of healing naturally from a large tumor — without drugs or surgery. Individuals from diverse cultures and all walks of life have embraced her work, as have many organizations throughout the world, from schools and children's shelters to hospices and clinics to prisons and addiction recovery centers. Her website is www.thejourney.com.

In addition, Brandon devotes a considerable amount of time and energy to our licensed international charity organization, Journey Outreach, bringing her healing and transformational work into the areas that need it most. This work is largely funded by Journey Seminars International and delegates of the work who wish to make a real difference in the world. If you would like to contribute, or to find out more about the work, please visit www.journeyoutreach.com.

JOURNEYWORK RESOURCES AND THE *FREEDOM IS* CD

If you enjoyed this book and found it beneficial, please pass it on to your friends and loved ones — we all deserve the experience of true freedom. And if you would like to know more about Journeywork or would like to roll up your sleeves and experience the more in-depth work at our regular seminars, workshops, and retreats, we encourage you to contact us. These events provide powerful and direct experiences of this work. They take place around the world and are presented live by Brandon or by her personally chosen and fully trained Journey presenters.

To enhance your experience of *Freedom Is*, we recommend that you use the companion CD, which includes recordings of all the book's guided meditations and process work. To order the companion CD or to find out more about Journey seminars and products, please contact Journeywork:

Tel: 1-866-860-0900 (Toll free in USA)
Tel: +1-973-680-0271 (From outside USA)
Email: usainfo@thejourney.com
Or check out our web site at:
www.thejourney.com.

NEW WORLD LIBRARY is dedicated to publishing books and other media that inspire and challenge us to improve the quality of our lives and the world.

We are a socially and environmentally aware company, and we make every attempt to embody the ideals presented in our publications. We recognize that we have an ethical responsibility to our customers, our employees, and our planet.

We serve our customers by creating the finest publications possible on personal growth, creativity, spirituality, wellness, and other areas of emerging importance. We serve our employees with generous benefits, significant profit sharing, and constant encouragement to pursue our most expansive dreams. As members of the Green Press Initiative, we print an increasing number of books with soy-based ink on 100 percent postconsumer waste recycled paper. Also, we power our offices with solar energy and contribute to nonprofit organizations working to make the world a better place for us all.

Our products are available
in bookstores everywhere.
For our catalog, please contact:

New World Library
14 Pamaron Way
Novato, California 94949

Phone: 415-884-2100 or 800-972-6657
Catalog requests: Ext. 50
Orders: Ext. 52
Fax: 415-884-2199

Email: escort@newworldlibrary.com
Website: www.newworldlibrary.com